UNDERSTANDING JOB SATISFACTION

UNDERSTANDING JOB SATISFACTION

Michael M. Gruneberg

A HALSTED PRESS BOOK

John Wiley & Sons
New York

First published 1979 by
THE MACMILLAN PRESS LTD
London and Basingstoke

Published in the U.S.A.
by Halsted Press, a Division
of John Wiley & Sons, Inc.

Printed in Great Britain

Library of Congress Cataloging in Publication Data

Gruneberg, Michael M
    Understanding job satisfaction.

    "A Halsted Press book."
    Bibliography: p.
    Includes index.
    1. Job satisfaction. 2. Job enrichment. I. Title.
HF5549.5.J63G78 1979   658.31'42   78–20782
ISBN 0–470–26610–4

To my late father, Rudi
To my mother, Vicki
   my wife Rhona
   my sons, Phillip and Leon
   my brother, Stephen

Contents

Preface

This book is intended to introduce the manager and the student to the complex topic of job satisfaction. No attempt therefore is made to cover the extensive research literature in detail and no attempt is made to cover every last aspect of the topic. Rather the intention of the book is to consider what job satisfaction is and how it might be improved, and to cover the major factors which affect and are affected by job satisfaction.

The first chapter introduces the topic and sets it in its historical context. Chapter 2 examines the theories which have been put forward to account for job satisfaction, including Herzberg's famous two-factor theory and theories of value fulfilment and equity. Chapters 3, 4 and 5 deal with factors which affect job satisfaction, including consideration of the importance of the work itself, and context factors such as pay, security, participation in decision-making and the social situation in which work takes place. Also considered are the effects which factors such as sex, age and education have on job satisfaction. Chapter 6 examines the consequences of job satisfaction and dissatisfaction, particularly the important question of the relationship between satisfaction and productivity, and the 'common sense' assumption of a direct relationship between job satisfaction and productivity is shown to be questionable. The chapter also considers the effects of job satisfaction on other factors of economic importance, such as absence and turnover, as well as on factors such as mental health. The final chapter examines ways of improving job satisfaction through the redesigning of jobs by techniques such as job enrichment. The evidence for job improvements through job enrichment is examined, limitations of the approach are pointed out, and steps indicated for the implementation of a job enrichment programme.

Of course, no introductory book on job satisfaction can cover all aspects and give the reader complete expertise in carrying out job improvement schemes. It is intended, however, that by the time the reader has finished the book, he will appreciate the major problems involved in the area and will be in a position to understand both the theoretical background to job redesign and its limitations, so that he can make an informed judgement on the relevance of the whole area of job satisfaction to his particular situation.

Acknowledgements

I should like to acknowledge the considerable help given me in the preparation of this manuscript by Dr David Oborne and Mr Stephen Gruneberg.

I should also like to thank Mrs Sue Oborne for her fortitude in typing the manuscript, and Mrs Maureen Rogers for help with the technical aspects.

July 1978   M. M. G.

1 Introduction

WHY STUDY JOB SATISFACTION?

Whilst there is no definitive list of the number of publications in the field of job satisfaction, there is little doubt that this is one of the most researched topics in psychology. A recent estimate by Locke (1976) suggested that over three thousand articles or dissertations have been produced to date, and the number is of course rising yearly. The reason for the popularity of the subject is not hard to explain. Most individuals spend a large part of their working lives at work, so that an understanding of factors involved in job satisfaction is relevant to improving the wellbeing of a large number of individuals in an important aspect of their lives. Another important reason for investigating job satisfaction is the belief that increasing job satisfaction will increase productivity and hence the profitability of organisations.

Over the last few years, however, the value of studying job satisfaction has come to be questioned. Lawler (1975), for example, questions whether wishing to increase the stock of human happiness in the world through improved job satisfaction is a sensible goal. He argues that dissatisfaction can be creative and lead to change of a constructive kind. Of what good, he asks, is the satisfaction of the cud-chewing cow, when man is capable of creativity and personal psychological growth? Whilst such a question does seem reasonable, it can also be argued that if the cud-chewing cow is happy, producing milk and satisfying the farmer, this is a reasonably desirable state of affairs. Not everyone, after all, longs to be creative and achieving in his own right. Some seek their satisfactions basically in the enjoyment of the company of others and it is a value judgement that this is an undesirable state of affairs.

A further criticism of the value of studying job satisfaction comes from those who see such research as providing little of worth. Davis and Cherns (1975), for example, write 'the altogether extraordinary emphasis on job satisfaction in the current and professional press appears to be adding to the confusion and apprehension, whilst not clarifying the fundamental issue . . . whether to change the means by which society gets its work done' (p. 14). In fact, this dissatisfaction arises because relationships between measures of job satisfaction and factors of economic importance such as productivity have often failed to materialise (see Chapter 6). Dissatisfaction also arises because it is felt that the current study of job satisfaction is 'the study of minimal satisfaction possible, under deprived conditions' (Davis, 1971).

Even though these objections to job satisfaction studies have some validity, it can nevertheless be argued that in such a complex area confusion will often arise, but that only considerable study will help to reduce this confusion; that a complex relationship such as that between job satisfaction and productivity requires subtle analysis; and that whatever the defects of present-day jobs, present-day realities are worthy of investigation. Indeed there is some evidence that however impoverished jobs seem to investigators, they are often seen as satisfactory to those carrying out the jobs. Hoppock (1935), for example, in his classic study, found less then a third of his sample to express themselves dissatisfied with their jobs, and Seashore (1975) reports that studies consistently find only 15–20 per cent of individuals to report themselves dissatisfied with their jobs.

DEFINITION AND MEASUREMENT OF JOB SATISFACTION

Perhaps the first question to ask in considering the question of job satisfaction is, what is it, and how is it measured? Most writers distinguish between job satisfaction and job morale. Morale refers to group wellbeing, whereas job satisfaction refers to the individual's emotional reactions to a particular job. Thus Locke (1976) defines job satisfaction as 'a pleasurable or positive emotional state, resulting from the appraisal of one's job or job experiences'. There is no one agreed definition, however, and Wanous and Lawler (1972) list nine different operational definitions, each based on a different theoretical orientation and each resulting in different measures. The major difference between definitions is in terms of the different ways in which aspects of job satisfaction are combined. When the relationship between job satisfaction for different aspects of the job and overall job satisfaction is analysed, considerable differences in the extent of the correlation are found. Wanous and Lawler also found three of the nine measures of satisfaction correlated significantly with absenteeism, whilst others did not. As the investigators conclude, 'had not a number of operational measures been used here, conclusions about the job satisfaction-absenteeism relationship would have been determined by the choice of which job satisfaction measures to use' (p. 103). Unfortunately, the data presented suggest that there is no optimal way to measure satisfaction. The best measure depends on what variable overall satisfaction is related to. Clearly, then, when considering research on job satisfaction, it is important to bear in mind just how complex is the interpretation of research findings, given the multiplicity of ways in which it can be conceived and measured. In Chapter 2 these theoretical positions will be considered.

Despite the diversity of measures, one measure, the Cornell Job Descriptive Index (JDI), is regarded by many workers as the most carefully developed instrument for measuring job satisfaction (Smith, Kendall and Hulin, 1969). The scale consists of five sub-scales for pay, promotion, people, supervision, and work, and each scale consists of a number of items. Whilst the scale is useful, and certainly it helps in the comparison of different studies when a common measure is used, tailor-made scales suffer from the drawback of not taking account of particular situations. For example, in order to understand areas of satisfaction and dissatisfaction of university teachers in a provincial university, Gruneberg and Startup (1978) had to take account of geographical characteristics of the particular institution studied as they involved problems peculiar to that institution. There is a conflict between investigating a particular situation and making the findings generalisable beyond one particular study.

The use of questionnaires of any kind to measure attitudes is, of course, problematic for a number of reasons. For example, it is well established that people often give socially acceptable rather than 'real' responses to questions, often expend little time and effort in filling them in and are often influenced by the way the questions are phrased. Furthermore, where not everyone returns the questionnaire, there is the problem of whether those who do return the questionnaire differ from those who do not. One might expect, for example, that those who do return a questionnaire are more interested in the subject being examined than those who do not. For all of these reasons, great care must be taken when considering job satisfaction studies based on questionnaires. Questionnaires should be regarded as instruments for approximating to the truth, rather than being an infallible means of measuring attitudes. Unfortunately, there are few, if any, alternatives which can give the same kind of information as questionnaires, as quickly or as economically. Methods of assessing attitudes such as interviewing are much more time-consuming, and suffer from the problem of biasing, introduced by the interviewer. Thus, the interviewer may cause the interviewee to make statements because the latter feels the interviewer will approve of them, rather than because they really reflect what the interviewee feels. No less than with questionnaire studies, therefore, care must be exercised in considering job satisfaction studies based on interviewing.

THE HISTORICAL BACKGROUND

As Weir (1976) points out, concern with fragmented, meaningless tasks has been expressed since the industrial revolution, when craftsmanship was replaced by machine-minding. Karl Marx was among those who pointed out that the fragmented nature of work resulted in a lack of fulfilment and gave rise to feelings of misery rather than enjoyment. Yet the initial concern of psychologists in industry was not basically with the psychological welfare of the individual, but with improvements in productivity as a result of changes in the physical environment. Foremost in this tradition was Frederick Taylor (1911). His famous study at the Bethlehem steelworks involved redesigning equipment and selecting the right men for the job, with a resultant increase in production. Unfortunately, it still remains true to this day that changes in job satisfaction *per se* have seldom been shown to have effects on production in the dramatic way illustrated by Taylor, or indeed to have much effect on absence.

The next development of historical importance was that of the Hawthorne studies begun in the 1920s, at the Hawthorne plant of the Western Electric Company, under the direction of Elton Mayo (see Roethlisberger and Dickson, 1939). The study began very much in the Taylor tradition, examining ways in which alterations in physical conditions would affect production. The first studies involved changes in the levels of illumination, and gave the surprising result that changes in illumination resulted in changes in productivity, whatever the direction of the change in illumination. Indeed, in one experiment, illumination was reduced to the level of moonlight, yet productivity increased. This finding has been attributed to individuals' increasing production because they were in an experimental situation. Perhaps they acted in this way because they felt the experimenters were taking an interest in them. Whatever the reason, when subjects in experiments improve performance, because of the experimental situation, this is now known as the 'Hawthorne' effect. The results of the studies on illumination led the Hawthorne investigators to set up other studies designed to examine why productivity should increase despite deteriorating physical conditions.

The first of these new studies, the relay assembly test room study, involved a small group of girls, all friendly towards each other. Rest pauses, hours of work, payment systems, heating and temperature were all varied and, after a two-year period, output had increased by 30 per cent. Clearly, in varying so many factors, it was difficult to establish exactly what had caused the increase in productivity, although the Hawthorne investigators considered it was mainly due to human associations at work. They based this conclusion on the fact that the work was carried out in a friendly atmosphere.

The role of friendly supervision as a factor in increased productivity is, unfortunately, of dubious validity. The first relay test room experiment began with girls who were friendly towards each other. However, talking became such a problem that two of the girls had to be dismissed! (Here is the red warning-light to the view that satisfaction with work and productivity are necessarily related!) Two replacement girls came in and immediately output increased, mainly due to the efforts of an Italian girl whose mother had died, leaving her the sole breadwinner. She immediately took a leadership role and led the way with increased productivity. Hence, productivity was certainly influenced by factors other than friendly supervision, indeed, friendly supervision came after an increase in productivity, rather than before.

Following the relay test room experiment, a number of other experiments were set up with the aim of clarifying the role of friendly supervision in increasing productivity. For a variety of reasons, however, they failed to demonstrate that social factors were critical in improving productivity. These reasons include the inadequacy of the experimental design and the difficulty of interpreting the reason for increased productivity in the context of the ongoing depression. Yet the experiment itself was of considerable historical importance in that it led directly to the 'Human Relations' school of thought in organisational psychology, which made the assumption that job satisfaction leads to increased productivity and that human relationships in organisations are the key to job satisfaction. Human relationships involve both leadership and supervisory behaviour, and informal social groups within organisations. How mistaken the assumption of a simple relationship between job satisfaction and productivity is, will be seen in Chapter 6. On the other hand, studies since Hawthorne have shown the importance of supervisory behaviour and of social relationships within work-groups on job satisfaction (see Chapter 4).

At the same time that Hawthorne was having its influence, Hoppock (1935) published his famous monograph on job satisfaction, perhaps the first major work to use survey methods and attitude scales in an examination of the problem. His work and orientation are perhaps typical of many studies which have taken place since, where job satisfaction is seen to consist of a multiplicity of factors. His approach typifies what has been termed the traditional approach to job satisfaction, in that he assumes that 'if the presence of a variable in the work situation leads to satisfaction, then its absence will lead to job dissatisfaction, and vice versa'.

One of Hoppock's studies involved analysing the responses of 500 teachers to a questionnaire on different aspects of their job. He examined differences between the hundred most and the hundred least satisfied. One factor which discriminated most was emotional maladjustment. Questions such as 'Do you feel sad or low spirited most of the time?' distinguished the least from the most satisfied group. He also found that 21 per cent of the least satisfied teachers had parents with unhappy marriages, compared with 6 per cent of the most satisfied teachers. Such findings are very much in line with more recent work on the relationship between job satisfaction and mental health, and on the relationship between job satisfaction and life satisfaction. The findings do suggest that to some extent individual factors will determine whether someone will be job satisfied or not.

Hoppock's discussion of the nature of job satisfaction also has relevance for present-day workers, given his finding that the majority of individuals in a small town reported themselves satisfied with their jobs. He raises the question of whether perhaps people are not too easily satisfied and suggests, as a possible reason for this, that individuals who stay in a job come to adapt to it. The fact that so many individuals report themselves satisfied even in dull, routine jobs, Hoppock sees as a hopeful sign. 'The effects of dissatisfaction, whatever they may be, are not the inevitable results of technological progress and the accompanying factory system. If two-thirds or more of the employed adults are not dissatisfied then there may be real hope for the remaining third.' Such a view is, of course, not likely to appeal to Davis (1971).

A major attack on earlier views of job satisfaction, such as those of Hoppock, was made by Herzberg in 1959. He attacked both the 'Human Relations' view that 'Human Relationships' were of critical importance in job satisfaction, and the traditional view that job satisfaction and dissatisfaction lay along a single continuum. Herzberg put forward his famous two-factor theory of job satisfaction, in which he argued that the causes of satisfaction and dissatisfaction were separate and distinct. Factors associated with the individual's needs for psychological growth contribute to job satisfaction. Such factors include the nature of the job and achievement. On the other hand, factors associated with job context, such as pay, and supervision, when they are defective, lead to job dissatisfaction. The emphasis on attaining job satisfaction through the work itself is perhaps the major interest of contemporary workers in the field of job satisfaction, although Herzberg's work has come in for considerable criticism. Because of the influence that Herzberg's theory still has on contemporary thinking, it will be discussed more fully in Chapter 2.

Few present-day workers would be willing to adhere to any one of the historical schools of job satisfaction. It is generally appreciated that the physical design of jobs can affect job satisfaction, as can social relationships, payment and supervisory systems and a myriad of other variables. Nor can generalisations be made without taking individuals' differences into account. At present, too, there is the tendency to take job satisfaction into account as one aspect only of the quality of working life.

2 Theoretical Considerations

Present-day theories of job satisfaction have been divided by Campbell *et al.* (1970) into two categories, content theories and process theories. Content theories give an account of the factors which influence job satisfaction; Maslow's (1943) Needs Hierarchy Theory and its development by Herzberg into the two-factor theory of job satisfaction will be considered under this heading.

Process theories try to give an account of the process by which variables such as expectations, needs and values interact with the characteristics of the job to produce job satisfaction. Equity theory, for example, argues that job satisfaction occurs when we compare what we put into a job and the rewards we receive with those of others, and find that we are equitably treated. The theory involves taking account of the expectations of individuals in relation to their job satisfaction. Reference group theory takes into account the way in which we refer to other individuals in deciding what is equitable. Need and value fulfilment theories account for job satisfaction in terms of the discrepancy between the individual's needs and values and what the job has to offer. The various theories are considered in turn.

CONTENT THEORIES

Maslow's Needs Hierarchy Theory

Perhaps the most popular account of job satisfaction at present is that job satisfaction involves fulfilling the individual's needs. One

9

of the first needs theories is that of Maslow (1943), who postulated a needs hierarchy, with needs divided into those of a lower order and those of a higher order. The needs are (1) basic physiological needs, (2) safety and security needs, (3) social (affection) needs, (4) esteem needs, and (5) self-actualisation needs. The first three are lower order needs and the fourth and fifth higher order needs. Maslow argues that only after the lower order needs are satisfied is man capable of being concerned with fulfilling higher order needs. An example of the application of the theory might be a man shipwrecked on a desert island. First he must find food and water to survive. Then follows a search for shelter and a means of establishing some defence for the shelter. Having done this, he will perhaps establish whether the island is inhabited, with a view to securing his own position and perhaps with a view to making social contact. Only after the basic needs are fulfilled is it possible to pay attention to the higher order needs of self-fulfilment, establishing his individual worth as a human being. In the job situation, the theory would predict that only after the lower order needs for security and pay have been satisfied will the employee seek satisfaction and achievement from the work itself.

Whilst the theory has great intuitive appeal, as Locke (1976) points out, it has some major drawbacks. First and foremost, there is no evidence for this hierarchy of needs, intuitively appealing as it might be. Again, it is in the nature of things that man's needs, even at the lowest levels, are not satisfied by one consummatory act. There are always physical needs to be satisfied. Indeed, there is some evidence that the satisfying of certain needs leads to a strengthening of those needs, rather than the reverse. Maslow did not, in fact, devise his theory in order to account for job satisfaction, but a number of theorists have used his theory in this way. Certainly, despite Lock's reservation, there is evidence that Maslow's theory is able to account for findings on occupational level and job satisfaction. Those in lower level occupations are likely to be motivated by lower order needs such as pay and security whereas those in higher level occupations who have these basic needs fulfilled are more interested in fulfilling higher order needs (see Centers and Bugental, 1966). It must be admitted, however, that other explanations are possible, such as the different expectations of individuals from different levels of society or education as to what a job should offer.

Herzberg's two-factor theory: The difference between satisfaction and dissatisfaction

Related to Maslow's needs hierarchy theory is Herzberg's famous two-factor theory of job satisfaction. Herzberg distinguishes two classes of factors involved in job satisfaction. The first group, motivators, are factors which, if present in the working situation, lead to satisfaction, but whose absence does not lead to dissatisfaction. Such factors include achievement, recognition and the intrinsic interest of the work itself, and correspond to the higher levels of 'self-autonomy' and 'self-actualisation' in Maslow's hierarchy of needs. These higher order factors are separate and distinct from the second group, hygiene factors, which, when inadequate, lead to job dissatisfaction, but which, when adequate, do not lead to job satisfaction. Among the hygiene factors are pay, security, and physical working conditions, and these correspond to the lower order needs in Maslow's hierarchy.

In splitting the factors involved in job satisfaction in this way, Herzberg argues that the causes of job satisfaction and job dissatisfaction are separate and distinct. An analogy might be with the concepts of pleasure and pain. For the normal healthy individual, the mere absence of pain is not pleasurable of itself, although over the short term, of course, it may be that the relief of pain is considered pleasurable. Similarly, hygiene factors such as working conditions do not normally lead to feelings of satisfaction when they are good, except in the short term when they are newly introduced. On the other hand, when they are bad, they do lead to job dissatisfaction.

The thrust of Herzberg's argument is that such factors as pay and working conditions are context factors which have little to do with deriving satisfaction from the job. They are necessary conditions for, but do not of themselves produce, job satisfaction.

On the other hand, job satisfaction is produced by the job itself allowing the individual to 'grow' psychologically, that is, to achieve a worthwhile aim, to achieve recognition for his efforts and so on, so that he can regard himself as a worthwhile individual. Herzberg argues that the absence of such motivators on the job does not, of itself, lead to dissatisfaction, but merely to a failure to achieve satisfaction.

Herzberg relates the concept of job satisfaction to the concept of mental health. Like job satisfaction and dissatisfaction, Herzberg argues that mental illness is not the obverse of mental health. The causes of mental illness are to be found in the strain imposed by the environment, whereas mental health involves reaction to factors involved in psychological growth. The mentally healthy individual will seek psychological growth from his job, and Herzberg (1966, p. 81) implies that those who seek satisfaction from hygiene factors have characteristics which add up to neurotic personalities.

Evidence for and against the theory

What, then, is the evidence for Herzberg's theory? The basic study reported in his book *The Motivation to Work* (1959), investigated engineers and accountants, and one criticism of Herzberg has been that his conclusions are based on far too narrow a sample of the working population. To be fair to Herzberg, however, a large number of studies using his technique of data collection have confirmed his findings, in general, for a great variety of samples. The basic technique employed by Herzberg is known as the critical incident technique in which workers are asked to think of a time when they felt exceptionally good or exceptionally bad about their present job or any other job they had had. These incidents were then classified and the results are shown in Diagram 1.

The results show clearly that the hypothesised motivators are given more frequently, but not exclusively, when talking of satisfying incidents. Similarly, the hypothesised hygiene factors are given more frequently, but not exclusively, when talking of

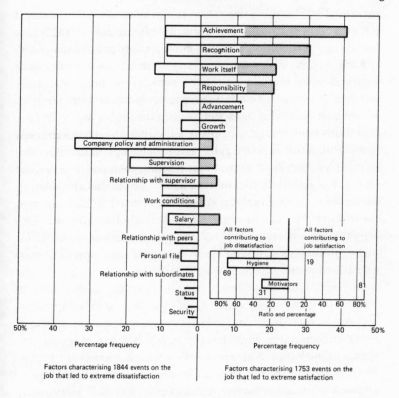

DIAGRAM 1. Motivating employees

feelings of dissatisfaction. Yet it is undoubtedly true that much of the controversy surrounding Herzberg's theory arises because of Herzberg's own ambiguity in interpreting the results. For example, on page 74 he states: 'When the factors involved in the job dissatisfaction events were coded, an entirely different set of factors evolved. These factors were similar to the satisfiers in their unidimensional effect. This time, however, they served only to bring about job dissatisfaction and were rarely involved in events that led to positive job attitudes.' Even a look at the diagram presented by Herzberg shows that the term 'rarely' in this context is highly suspect. 'Salary', for example, extends considerably into 'satisfiers', 'recognition' extends considerably into 'dissatisfiers'.

King (1970) and Gardner (1977), in reviewing the work undertaken on Herzberg's theory, take up the point about the ambiguous way in which Herzberg states his theoretical position. King lists five possible interpretations of the theory, from the view that motivators contribute only to satisfaction and hygienes only to dissatisfaction (Theory 1, the 'strong' theory), to the view that motivators contribute more to satisfaction than do hygienes and vice versa for dissatisfaction (Theory 5, the 'weak' theory). Certainly even on Herzberg's own results, it is difficult to see how the strong theory can be maintained. It might be added that such attempts have been made by arguing that satisfiers 'in the wrong place' are due to sampling error, but such a position does seem difficult to justify.

In fact, Herzberg does indicate that he allows for the possibility that some individuals do gain satisfaction from hygiene factors. Those individuals are regarded by Herzberg as being unfortunates who 'have not reached the stage of personality development at which self-actualising needs are active'. From this point of view they are fixated at a less mature level of personal adjustment (p. 80), and again (p. 81), 'a hygiene seeker is not merely a victim of circumstances, but is motivated in the direction of temporary satisfaction'.

Two comments are perhaps in order at this point. First, even in Herzberg's own work, hygiene factors are sometimes reported as leading to actual satisfaction. The general statement, therefore, that only motivators satisfy must be qualified. Second, Herzberg equates hygiene seekers with poor adjustment, but there is ample evidence (e.g. Kasl, 1973) that poor working conditions can also lead to bad adjustment. Indeed, it could well be argued that in the many situations where psychological growth is not possible on the job, because it is dull and routine, a search for hygiene factors such as money is a healthy adjustment and in no way indicative of a neurotic personality. Furthermore, many studies have shown that it is not only the individual, but the culture from which the individual comes, which determines what he will seek from his job, and for some groups, money is seen as the most important aspect of the job. To take account of one's social relationship is not normally considered poor adjustment.

Locke too (1976) takes issue with Herzberg's ideas on mental health. He points out that lack of self-esteem, rather than failure to cope with hygiene factors, seems to be a major factor in neurosis. Certainly, this part of Herzberg's theory is written with little regard for evidence and constitutes a weak part of the argument.

Besides this criticism, a large number of theorists have challenged Herzberg's theories on a number of other issues. One of the most serious charges is that Herzberg's theory is method-bound, that is, when using his method, the critical incident technique, the results tend to confirm the weak form of his theory at least. Using other methods, however, there have been consistent failures to confirm Herzberg's theory. The main argument against the critical incident technique is that it may induce respondents to blame unsatisfactory events on others, for example, their supervisor (hygiene factor), whilst taking credit themselves for the good things that happen, for example, claiming responsibility (motivator). Herzberg denies this by arguing that in fact when employees wish to make themselves look good they do sometimes blame motivators, saying they have no responsibility, uninteresting work and so on. Herzberg's central argument is that the incidence of this kind of response is much less than is the response of dissatisfaction caused by hygiene factors. Actually, this argument of Herzberg's can be turned round and used to disprove the 'strong' theory of the two-factor model, which claims that only hygiene factors contribute to job dissatisfaction.

Another problem with the critical incident technique is that bad motivators may not occur as critical incidents. Being bored with one's job, for example, is not something that necessarily occurs at a critical point in time, it occurs from day to day. There is often, in other words, no incident which makes the job boring, it is merely the repetition of what has gone before. Unless it can be shown that the aspects of motivators which cause dissatisfaction can be captured equally well by the critical incident technique, then, as King (1970) points out, other methods of establishing Herzberg's theory are required. However, attempts to verify Herzberg's theory using other techniques, as was noted earlier, have met with almost universal failure.

Herzberg, it must be pointed out, was well aware of the possibility of methodological criticism of the critical incident technique. His reason for using the technique in the first place was the mistrust shown by a large number of psychologists of job satisfaction questionnaires, for the kind of reason discussed in Chapter 1. Unfortunately, the fact that there are problems with other techniques does not necessarily lessen the problems of Herzberg's own technique.

An important point concerning Herzberg's theory is that he does not say how the motivators and hygienes will be weighted together to give an overall assessment of job satisfaction. In essence, he claims only that motivators contribute to job satisfaction, and hygienes to dissatisfaction, and says nothing about overall job satisfaction. An analogy again might be with pleasure and pain. Herzberg's argument is that the kind of things which cause pleasure, such as falling in love, are separate and distinct from the kind of things which cause pain, such as breaking one's leg. How a person who has fallen in love and has broken a leg in the same week would feel if he were asked whether or not he was happy, cannot be deduced from the theory. Thus as Bochman (1971) has pointed out, studies which have sought to disprove Herzberg's theories by relating motivators and hygiene factors to overall job satisfaction, can be seen to be irrelevant to the argument. Of course, exactly how individuals weigh up what is satisfying and what is dissatisfying in coming to a decision about overall job satisfaction is a very important issue. Indeed, it might be regarded as *the* issue in measuring the degree to which an individual is or is not satisfied with his job. To the extent that Herzberg plays down this problem, his theory is weak in giving an account of the nature of job satisfaction.

A second point of major importance in considering Herzberg's theory is the distinction between being 'satisfied with' and 'deriving satisfaction from' one's job. Herzberg's theory is clearly concerned with the latter, yet questionnaires which ask respondents to rate on a scale from 'satisfied' to 'dissatisfied' with various aspects of their job, are asking for the former. An example might help to clarify the difference. As I write, I am very satisfied with my desk, it is made of nice wood, it has many drawers, it does not wobble, and it allows me room to spread my papers around. Yet I derive no job satisfaction from it. I do not arrive in the morning, look at my desk, beam with joy, caress the top and sigh gently – I don't even notice it. On the other hand, if it were to wobble, crack down the centre or prove too small, it would undoubtedly be a cause for annoyance and concern – a cause of job dissatisfaction. In Herzberg's terms, my desk is purely a hygiene factor, a means by which intrinsic aspects of the work can be carried out. No amount of improvement of the desk will contribute to my deriving satisfaction from the job. Thus only questionnaires which ask respondents questions such as, 'how much do you derive satisfaction from . . . ?' are relevant tests of Herzberg's theory in relation to satisfaction. It is clear too, from the example, that Herzberg's theory has intuitive appeal; it does seem reasonable to suppose that some aspects of the job are only dissatisfying if they are defective, but not satisfying if they are adequate.

Yet to point out one hygiene factor as not contributing to job satisfaction, cannot be regarded as a refutation of the considerable evidence that for some individuals, hygiene factors such as pay are a source of satisfaction. As noted above, even Herzberg's own data indicate this, and various other studies support the view that certain hygiene factors can contribute to job satisfaction, and more importantly, certain motivators can contribute to dissatisfaction, as Herzberg (p. 131) allows. Studies such as those of Wall and Stephenson (1970), would seem to indicate that motivators are more important factors in both job satisfaction and job dissatisfaction than are hygiene factors. This, certainly, is the position taken by many current workers in the field, e.g. Warr and Wall (1975), and would certainly be most consistently supported by relevant studies, except those using the critical incident technique.

Whilst few people, therefore, appear to allow that Herzberg has provided evidence which unambiguously supports his theory, there is little doubt that his emphasis on the importance of motivators rather than hygiene factors as contributing to job satisfaction is justified and has wide acceptance (e.g. Locke, 1976). Furthermore, his argument that those who do gain satisfaction from hygiene rather than motivator factors are missing out on life is readily accepted by researchers, such as Locke, who see such individuals having values which conflict with their real needs. One might argue, however, that in reality the present opportunities for psychological growth on the job are so limited and confined to so few people that it is perhaps fortunate that so many seek only hygiene satisfaction from the job.

In conclusion, it must not be thought that Herzberg regards the adequate provision of hygiene factors as unimportant – prevention of pain is as important in its way as the provision of pleasure. In its way, ensuring adequate hygiene factors is as essential for wellbeing at work as are motivators. Indeed, Herzberg argues that it is only when hygiene factors such as pay are adequate that one can begin to structure a job so that motivators come to play a part in the individual's satisfaction with his job.

Herzberg's emphasis on intrinsic aspects of the job is in part a healthy reaction to the 'Human Relations' school, which saw human relationships at work as the central area of concern for organisational psychology. Whatever the defects of Herzberg's theory, thanks to Herzberg, no one will ever again be able to ignore the importance of analysing characteristics of the work itself in coming to an understanding of job satisfaction.

PROCESS THEORIES

As previously noted, the theories of Maslow and Herzberg have been described by Campbell *et al.* (1970) as content theories of job satisfaction, since they are basically interested in identifying the factors which make for job satisfaction and dissatisfaction. In contrast there are a number of theories called process theories, which aim to describe the interaction between variables in their relationship to job satisfaction.

Process theorists see job satisfaction as being determined, not only by the nature of the job and its context, but by the needs, values and expectations that individuals have in relation to their job. For example some individuals have a greater need for achievement than others and where a job gives no opportunity for achievement, such individuals are likely to be more frustrated than those whose need is less. Process theories, no less than Herzberg's theory of job satisfaction, thus attack the view that increases in job satisfaction simply arise by giving individuals more of a variable that normally leads to satisfaction – for example, more money. If an individual expects a £10.00 pay rise, then a rise of £5.00 might well be positively dissatisfying. Yet whilst all process theorists agree that job satisfaction depends on the relationship between the individual and his work environment, there are considerable differences of view as to which process relates to job satisfaction. At least three classes of theory have been put forward; that job satisfaction is determined by the extent of the discrepancy between what the job offers and what the individual expects; what the individual needs; and what the individual values.

EXPECTATIONS AND EQUITY THEORY

That expectations about our environment affect how we behave is of course well known to everyone. I remember, for example, meeting my mother very unexpectedly on a train 400 miles from home, and being too embarrassed to say 'Hullo Mum' in case it was not really her. Fortunately my mother was certain she recognised me! One important aspect of expectations is that they give to the individual a frame of reference by which he judges the world about him. If events in the world do not fit his frame of reference, he is often unhappy and sometimes changes his interpretation of the world in order to accommodate awkward facts. In a job, we use frames of reference when deciding, for example, what is reasonable pay. We relate what we are getting to what others are getting and if we find ourselves getting too little, we become dissatisfied. This is the central notion of equity theory which argues that we have a concept of what is just reward for our efforts. There is, as it were, a psychological contract between employer and employee, that for a given amount of effort, there should be a given amount of reward. This is established by the individual comparing the efforts and rewards he receives with those of others. Only where the rewards and efforts are seen as reasonable in terms of the rewards of other people is there satisfaction.

What, then, happens when there is a discrepancy between the individual's effort and reward, and those of others? According to equity theory, the employee may well put less into his work, take extended coffee breaks, give poorer quality production and so on. He might decide to withdraw from the situation or he might change his expectations to be more in line with what he is receiving. Certainly the evidence of Lawler and O'Gara (1967), for example, is that when underpaid, individuals behave so as to increase outcomes but to reduce inputs. Subjects in their experiment increased the quantity but reduced the quality of their work in order to increase payments for less input. Other studies have confirmed that under-reward leads to dissatisfaction (see Pritchard, Dunnette and Jorgenson, 1972).

What if the individual is given a higher reward than he feels is equitable? Equity theorists would predict that this too would cause dissatisfaction. In reviewing the literature on overpayment, Pritchard, Dunnette and Jorgenson (1972) regard the evidence as at best limited. A number of studies have failed to find any effect of over-reward, although one of Pritchard *et al.*'s studies did suggest that over-reward led to dissatisfaction.

When individuals are overpaid, it is likely that they will develop 'coping mechanisms' so that they can accept excessive payments without too many qualms. It is not improbable, for example, that employees who are overpaid will quickly reconcile themselves to the state of affairs. Pritchard (1969) argues that in industrial situations, where there is overpayment, individuals will feel that others are underpaid and that it is the fault of the system. Certainly it seems intuitively likely that it is easier to live with a situation in which one is overpaid compared to one in which one is underpaid.

The evidence on equity theory is clearly not straightforward. It appears able to account for some aspects of satisfaction but not others. Locke (1976) argues that the problem with equity theory is not so much that it has been shown to be wrong but that it is so loose that it is able to account for anything.

REFERENCE GROUP THEORY

As noted above, an essential aspect of equity theory is that the individual compares his inputs and outputs from a job with those of others, such as his friends, his work-mates, people in his industry and so on, before deciding whether or not he is equitably treated. Many theorists, such as Hulin and Blood (1968), have argued that an understanding of the groups to whom the individual relates (reference group) is therefore of critical importance in understanding job satisfaction.

A study of Klein and Maher (1966) suggests the importance of reference groups. They found that college-educated managers were less satisfied with their pay than non-college-educated managers. It is suggested that part of the explanation is that college-educated managers have higher expectations of pay because of their education and that they related their salary to a different reference group, namely a highly educated and highly paid group, compared to those of non-college-educated managers who compared their salaries with other non-college-educated and lower paid individuals.

As Korman (1977) points out, however, reference group theory leaves many questions unanswered. How, for example, do individuals choose which reference group to relate to? Why do reference groups have the expectations they do? What constitutes a reference group? Clearly individuals differ in the reference group they choose because of their own individual personalities. Newcombe (1958), for example, in his famous study of attitude change amongst girls from conservative backgrounds entering a liberal American college, found that whilst many girls took on the liberal views in vogue in the college, a number of girls took their parents as reference points and remained conservative in outlook. Such girls often appeared isolated and unable to relate to other students, and it may be that they were basically insecure individuals. On the other hand, Korman suggests that those most influenced by their reference groups are those with low self-esteem. Those with high self-esteem can afford to ignore the reference group to a larger extent and 'do their own thing'. At present the only certainty is that reference group theory is at best a partial explanation of how individuals regard the inputs and rewards of the job as equitable.

It is clear, therefore, that expectations based on reference groups must be supplemented by a knowledge of personality factors and of individual needs and values in any assessment of what the individual considers equitable in relation to his job satisfaction. Locke (1976), for example, has questioned whether expectations and their relationship to what the job actually gives, have any relevance to understanding job satisfaction. He argues that when expectations and reality are different the reaction is not dissatisfaction, but surprise. Satisfaction or dissatisfaction will depend upon the value which we place on our reward. For example, we might well be dissatisfied with an expected dismissal or an expected demotion and be extremely satisfied with an unexpected pay rise or promotion. This is not an entirely convincing argument, however, as one might be *more* satisfied with an unexpected promotion and *more* dissatisfied with an unexpected dismissal, than when such events are expected.

Certainly, experimental evidence exists to suggest that when one changes expectations without changing values, then there are no effects on reported satisfaction. Amaee and Gruneberg (1976) found that university students on entering university are very lacking in knowledge concerning the role of the university lecturer. In the majority of cases students are unaware of the importance of research and administration as functions of the university teacher. Consequently, they tend to consider that he spends far longer in the role of undergraduate teacher than he does. Amaee (1978) then examined the effect on the degree of expressed satisfaction with teaching, of giving students realistic information on the role of their lecturers. Students were informed that lecturers were not normally formally qualified to teach, that they had other functions such as research and administration which were of importance to the adequate functioning of the university, and that time for undergraduate teaching and contact was thus limited for those reasons. Measures of values, expectations and satisfaction with various aspects of the teaching process were measured before and after the information was given. The results showed that whilst there were considerable changes in expectations concerning the teacher's role, there was little discernible change in the satisfaction with, or the perceived value of the teaching. This of course, is not really surprising. University students come to university to obtain a degree, for which teaching is an essential aspect. Finding that their teachers are not trained to teach and have other functions to perform may change their expectations concerning the quality of teaching they receive. It is hardly likely to change their feelings concerning how well teaching fulfills the important role to them of enabling the student to acquire a good degree. To this extent, therefore, the findings of Amaee support Locke in emphasising the importance of values rather than expectations.

There are, however, a number of studies (e.g. Scott, 1972 and Wanous, 1973), which indicate that giving individuals a more realistic idea (i.e. more realistic expectations) of the institution they join and the role they will be playing has a positive effect on job satisfaction. It is possible, however, that this is because the information given is redirecting the attention of employees from values that cannot be fulfilled on the job, to values which they did not realise could be fulfilled. Giving realistic information may also function to clarify the roles people are expected to play in the organisation. Ambiguity of role is one factor reported to cause job dissatisfaction (see Chapter 4).

Expectations are also likely to affect job satisfaction where they affect self-esteem. A junior manager who fails to gain the post of managing director of General Electric may well be less dissatisfied with his failure than a failure to obtain a junior management job elsewhere. Even though he values the managing director's job more than the junior job, his self-esteem is likely to suffer less if he fails to obtain the more prestigious appointment. Thus expectations rather than values would determine job satisfaction in this situation.

A further important aspect of expectation noted by equity theory but ignored by Locke is that certain expectations have intrinsic value for the individual. For example, the expectation that in Great Britain cars are driven on the left-hand side of the road is of value to the individual in predicting other people's behaviour. We all have expectations, within limits, of how people are going to behave in practically every social situation, and it is these expectations which enable us to behave in a social way. The expectations that we have about situations are valuable to the individual in giving stability to his environment. The act of undermining our expectations, therefore, can be dissatisfying.

Clearly, the problem of expectations in relation to job satisfaction is complex. In some situations, changes in expectations appear to lead to changes in job satisfaction, in others not. It may be that changes in expectations lead only to changes in job satisfaction where there are accompanying shifts in values expected, or it may be that the fulfilment of certain expectations has a value in its own right. What is quite clear is that a knowledge of the expectations of individuals in relation to their job is of considerable significance in an understanding of how people behave in their jobs.

NEEDS/VALUE FULFILMENT THEORIES

Whatever the role of expectations in job satisfaction, it has been noted that it cannot be the whole story. Individuals differ in what they value in a job and this, too, is likely to affect the degree to which they are satisfied. Kuhlin (1963), for example, conducted a study on the job satisfaction of schoolteachers. He found that male teachers wanted far more from their job in terms of achievement than did female teachers. The discrepancy between what men wanted from the job and what they got was related more to overall job satisfaction than was the discrepancy for women, for whom the job was not such an important aspect of life satisfaction. However, each individual clearly differs in what he wants from a job, and the aim of need discrepancy theorists is to examine the way such differences operate in relation to job satisfaction. Thus a number of theorists have argued that it is the degree to which the job fulfils needs that determines job satisfaction.

Vroom (1964) has examined two forms of the need fulfilment theory. The first, the subtractive model, argues that job satisfaction is negatively related to the degree of discrepancy between what the individual needs and the extent to which the job supplies these needs. The greater the total discrepancy, counting all needs, the less the satisfaction; the greater the congruence, the greater the satisfaction. One problem with this theory is that it ignores the importance of a particular need. For example, if I have only a moderate need for exercise gratification on my job, say, one unit, and the job provides one unit, then I shall be as satisfied with this (there being no discrepancy between need and fulfilment) as I shall be if I have a strong need for achievement, say ten units, which is also fulfilled by the job providing ten units of fulfilment. Thus, a view of job satisfaction which does not take into account the relative importance of needs is misleading. Some needs are more important to individuals than others, so that a fulfilment of such needs can well be set off against minor failures to fulfil lesser needs. On the other hand, a failure to fulfil important needs may well not be set off by satisfaction with a whole host of minor needs. The study of Kuhlin shows the subtractive model is related to overall job satisfaction for males but not for females. Since individual differences affect the importance of needs and need fulfilment on the job, it would appear that the subtractive model is, at best, only a partial answer.

Vroom therefore argues for a second model, the multiplicative model, of need fulfilment. In this form of the need fulfilment theory, need importance is taken into account by multiplying the perceived amount of need fulfilment offered by the job, by the importance to the individual of that need. The products for each need are then added together to give a total measure of job satisfaction. Suppose, for example, that a person receives five units of achievement from his job and thinks that it has seven units of importance, then the five is multiplied by seven to give thirty-five units. All the other need fulfilments on the job are calculated in the same way, and all are added together to give a total sum. So if an individual has eighty units, he will be more satisfied with his job than someone with sixty units. Vroom found support for this type of model from studies in which only individuals who liked to take part in decision-making were affected in their job satisfaction by whether or not their supervisor was participative.

Yet as Locke (1976) points out, even the multiplicative model of job satisfaction has its problems. It fails to distinguish between how much one wants something (its importance) and how much of something one wants. For example, I might want a salary of £12000, but being realistic, not want it very much. Alternatively, I may very much wish to serve on the University Senate, but only for a short period of time. As Locke points out, in measuring discrepancy, people may be influenced by value; and in measuring value, people may be influenced by the discrepancy between what they want and what the job offers. It would therefore be highly desirable if the amount of a value wanted and how much a person wants a value could be distinguished.

Nevertheless, need fulfilment models of job satisfaction have intuitive appeal. Locke, however, is unhappy with the term 'needs' and prefers to argue that it is what we value that is important. After all, we often value things which we do not need, or which are indeed positively harmful to us, such as drugs. For most theorists, however, the terms 'need' and 'value' are used more or less synonymously.

TEMPORAL CHANGES IN JOB SATISFACTION

One criticism of job satisfaction studies is that they tend to be static, taking a picture of job satisfaction at one point in time, rather than examining how job satisfaction changes and how job values change in the course of the individual's lifetime. Job satisfaction is regarded by some theorists as a constant adaptation to changing situations and changing values. For example, what might constitute a factor of psychological growth, a motivator, at one point in time, might merely become a hygiene factor at another point in time. The new bride might be regarded as a motivator who stimulates the young man in a positive way. After fifteen years or so of marriage, the positive stimulation may be lacking but the stability, care and love provided give pleasurable feelings of security so that threats to the relationship still have unhappy consequences. In other words, the wife has become a hygiene factor! Similarly a job might involve a number of facets, some of which start out as exciting but soon become a matter of routine. The university teacher initially enjoys reading essays. After a few years, however, rarely does it fill him with pleasurable anticipation.

Whilst changes in job satisfaction with age have been reported frequently (see Chapter 5), only recently have theorists tried to understand the dynamics of job satisfaction changes over time. Van Maanen and Katz (1976) present one of the first attempts to look at this problem. They regard job satisfaction in terms of three distinct areas; the organisational policies aspect (pay, conditions, etc.); the interpersonal context of the job; and the job itself. They presented a job satisfaction questionnaire to four occupational groups: administrative and professional workers (both groups having career structures), and clerical and main-tenance workers (who had no career structures).

Their major finding was of considerable differences between jobs in their reported satisfaction with different aspects, over time. Administrators, for example, displayed a sharp increase in satisfaction with company and policy decisions after ten years, a pattern absent in other groups. Not only does this indicate that changes in job satisfaction do not necessarily occur only shortly after joining an organisation, but can take place a considerable time after, it also indicates the dangers in generalising from one group to another. As Van Maanen and Katz point out, the finding of increased satisfaction with company policy after a period of ten years is perhaps not surprising as administrators will be increasingly involved in these company policies as time goes on. As far as other job properties are concerned, administrators' satisfaction with interaction falls after a year or so, getting back to its initial level only after about twenty years. Perhaps this too is not surprising, since administrators have to make decisions which affect other people's lives and often lead to inter-personal conflict. The third area, the actual job itself, grows rapidly in terms of satisfaction for the first year or two, then stays at this higher level. Presumably getting to know and mastering the job leads to a higher level of satisfaction. Generally, however, the actual overall level of satisfaction falls below that of satisfaction with the job itself, indicating possibly the importance of context (hygiene) factors in the assessment of overall job satisfaction of administrators.

As with administrators, professional employees show long-term changes in level of satisfaction. In particular, there appears to be a decrease in satisfaction with the job itself after a period of about fifteen years, accompanied by a sharp drop in overall satisfaction, which recovers after about twenty years. Satisfaction with interaction with employees, after decreasing for the first two years, steadily increases over time, whilst satisfaction with company policies, after decreasing, increases after about ten years. The overall satisfaction of professionals appears little better after twenty-five years than after two. This is contrary to the pattern for clerical and maintenance workers, which is characterised by a constant climb in overall job satisfaction with time, despite the fact that the occupations have no career stages. The puzzling aspect of these findings is that overall job satisfaction is consistently higher than is satisfaction with any of the components (for example, satisfaction with the job itself, interaction with others, or organisational policies). These start at a low level and then decline further after about fifteen years in the case of the clerical workers. Such findings, if they really do reflect the actual situation, tend to suggest an increasing adjustment to the work situation despite perceived difficulties with the job, for clerical workers.

Whilst the study by Van Maanen and Katz involved a survey of some 4400 individuals, it must be stressed that the findings are of limited value, as they surveyed individuals at different stages of tenure in occupations at one point in time, rather than examining the individual's progress in his career at different points in time. The methodological problems inherent in studies of the kind carried out by Van Maanen and Katz are enormous. Those who leave an occupation may well be different from those who stayed, in terms of their satisfaction with the job. Again, the turnover rate in different occupations is probably different so that measuring the responses of those who have lasted twenty-five years in different occupations is bound to be subject to distortion. Again, over the years the intake to different occupations may change in terms of cultural background. For example, many more people now go to university in Britain than was the case twenty-five years ago and they therefore tend to have to enter occupations they would not have considered had they been born twenty-five years earlier. The Van Maanen and Katz study is therefore at best a guideline, of very limited scope, but nevertheless, in pointing out the possibilities of important findings using a longitudinal approach, undoubtedly important. Our basic assumptions about job design and career structure may at best be inadequate, at worst wrong. How our job satisfaction interacts with our personality development and life and family situation over time is unknown, yet likely to be of crucial importance. How jobs which start off interesting (motivators) become routine, how their interest can be sustained and who is likely to benefit in the long term from job design changes – all these problems are in urgent need of examination. Without an understanding of this dimension of job satisfaction, theories of job satisfaction are incomplete.

SUMMARY

There are basically two classes of theory of job satisfaction. First, those which attempt to give an account of what needs, values or expectations are important to individuals in determining their degree of job satisfaction (content theories). Second, theories which, in general terms, try to give an account of how the individual's needs, values and expectations interact with the job to provide job satisfaction and dissatisfaction (process theories).

An analysis of the content theories of Maslow and Herzberg reveals many major methodological and conceptual problems. As far as Maslow's needs hierarchy theory is concerned, it is postulated we have needs in ascending order from the basic physiological and security needs to the higher order needs of autonomy and self-actualisation. No real evidence exists to support the theory, intuitively appealing as it might be. Herzberg's theory, which postulates that the causes of satisfaction and dissatisfaction are separate and distinct, can be related to Maslow's needs hierarchy theory. Thus, those factors which cause dissatisfaction when not satisfied are the lower level needs of Maslow's hierarchy, those factors which cause satisfaction when satisfied involve the higher order needs. Again, as with Maslow, the major problem with Herzberg's theory is that the evidence, apart from that obtained by means of the critical incident technique, does not support the theory. The critical incident technique is clearly suspect and studies using other techniques strongly support the view that motivators are important both in satisfaction and dissatisfaction. The evidence on dissatisfaction is perhaps not so clear cut, although here too, it does appear that some individuals derive satisfaction from hygiene factors such as pay, whether it is 'good' for them or not.

Whatever the merits, or otherwise, of Herzberg's theory, it is undoubtedly of great historical importance in shifting the emphasis of interest in job satisfaction away from the 'human relations' school's concern with human contacts at work, to the importance of the job itself as crucial to an understanding of job satisfaction. Moreover, Herzberg has been a prime instigator of the movement to redesign jobs in order to allow individuals to have possibilities of psychological growth.

One of the major criticisms of Herzberg is that he plays down the importance of individual differences in coming to an understanding of job satisfaction and it is here that the process theories of job satisfaction have an important contribution to make. They claim that it is the interaction between the individual's expectations, needs and values and what the job offers which gives rise to satisfaction and dissatisfaction. Merely looking at the job itself, therefore, in terms of opportunities for psychological growth, is a mistake, without looking at the individual who is to fill the job and who will vary in terms of the values he wishes fulfilled in the job.

Exactly how the individual interacts with the job is, however, the subject of dispute. Some theorists argue that it is the matching of an individual's expectations to what the job offers which determines job satisfaction. Where expectations are not fulfilled, there will be job dissatisfaction. Whilst this kind of theory has support when the job does not come up to expectations, it does not seem to be supported when the job exceeds expectations. Equity theory, an extension of this kind of theorising, argues that job satisfaction arises when the individual compares what he puts in to a job and what he gets out of a job, with other people's inputs and outputs. Where he regards his rewards as being equitable compared to other people, he is satisfied, where he feels they are inequitable, he is dissatisfied.

How the individual comes to compare himself with others is the concern of the reference group theorists. They point to the importance of peer groups in determining what the individual regards as reasonable to expect from his job in terms of reward, and what is reasonable to give in terms of effort. Yet as Korman points out, reference group theory is as yet unable to specify why some individuals choose one reference group whereas other apparently similar individuals choose another. Personality factors must, therefore, be an important aspect of understanding the kind of rewards and efforts that an individual seeks and expects on a job. Again, as Locke (1976) points out, expectations that individuals have do not necessarily determine job satisfaction. For example, one can be satisfied with an unexpected promotion or dissatisfied with an expected dismissal. Individual needs and values, just as much as expectations, determine whether or not an individual will be satisfied or dissatisfied with a job. Expectations may, nevertheless, be of critical importance in job satisfaction by determining which values and needs the individual is going to seek to satisfy in the job situation. Furthermore, a framework of expectations may well have considerable value for the individual in giving stability to the job situation.

Process theorists such as Vroom have tried to account for job satisfaction in terms of matching individual needs to what the job provides. Two models are considered, the subtractive and the multiplicative, but both have their limitations. As far as the subtractive model is concerned, it fails to take account of the importance of different needs. As far as the multiplicative model is concerned, it fails to distinguish how much a need is wanted and how much of the need is wanted.

Finally, in considering any theory of job satisfaction, the changing values and adaptations that individuals make over time must be taken into account. Job satisfaction research has largely given a picture of job satisfaction as something static, but as Davis and Cherns (1975) point out, job satisfaction involves a dynamic interaction between the individual and his environment. The work of Van Maanen and Katz, despite its limitations, supports this view.

Whatever the differences and limitations of using one approach, it seems clear that job satisfaction involves the matching of the individual's needs, values and expectations to what the job offers. In such a complex field as job behaviour, it is likely that no single theory accounts for all the phenomena all the time. Sometimes expectations, sometimes values, will be the main focus of interest; sometimes examining the individual's personality, sometimes examining the cultural background, will be the most fruitful approach. Certainly, at present we are far from a generally acceptable overall theory.

3 Job Satisfaction and the Job Itself

In the last chapter it was pointed out that investigators of job satisfaction have not always been interested in the nature of the job itself. Instead, their interest, until relatively recently, has been in trying to improve the social relationships and social situation of people in relatively poor work situations. It was the writings of Herzberg in 1959 which drew attention to the view that to increase job satisfaction one had to change the actual job being done. Such a self-evident view has an assumption which has only recently been accepted as valid, namely that individuals have a right to expect satisfaction from their jobs. Whilst some authors look nostalgically back to the days of the skilled craftsman, it is often forgotten that such craftsmen were rare in comparison with those for whom backbreaking work was the order of the day. Present concern with enriching jobs and gaining satisfaction from the work itself took second place to concern with physical loads and meagre financial returns. As Behling (1964) notes, dissatisfaction with work is neither new nor strictly a product of the modern form of work organisation. 'For by far the greatest percentage of every previous culture it was the normal part of their daily lives. Rather than creating dissatisfaction with work, progressive manufacturing has merely changed the source of dissatisfaction' (p. 15).

Behling goes on to argue, using Maslow's hierarchy of needs, that with a fulfilling of the lower level needs for security and with a reduction of physical demands at work, it is only now that attention has been focused on the satisfaction inherent in the work itself.

Dissatisfaction at work then, is neither new, nor is it the product of the twentieth century. What modern industry has done is to focus attention on a new set of problems, and to give rise to expectations of satisfaction at work, which previously were the prerogative of the few.

This chapter will examine factors related to satisfaction with the job itself. Perhaps the most important of these are the attainment of success and recognition, the application of skills, the feeling of doing something worthwhile and involvement in one's job.

SUCCESS AND JOB SATISFACTION

The relationship between success in a task and satisfaction has been examined by Locke (1965). He notes the difficulty in deciding upon the cause-effect relationship, particularly if one asks individuals after the event how satisfied they were with the task. The most successful might report themselves satisfied because of their success, when in fact, it was their enjoyment of the task which led to greater effort and hence greater success (achievement). In other words, satisfaction may *cause* greater achievement rather than be caused by it. Locke's own experiments involved students solving problems of various degrees of difficulty and his results indicated, at each level of difficulty, a clear relationship between degree of success and the extent of liking the task.

When asked for the reasons for satisfaction or dissatisfaction with their tasks, those who were satisfied gave as the main reason 'feelings of improvement' whilst those dissatisfied with the task gave reasons such as 'boredom'. This study suggests, therefore, that the successful completion of the task caused feelings of satisfaction. Further suggestive evidence that success causes satisfaction comes from a study by Gebhard (1948) who found evidence of increased liking for tasks for which there had been previous success. Despite the methodological difficulties which make the interpretation of the causal relationship difficult to assess, it appears probable that satisfaction increases with success.

Locke also raises the question of exactly what is meant by 'success' in a task. It could, of course, mean the actual completion of a task set by someone else, but this need not necessarily be the case. An individual may set his own standards, in terms of his own competence, and feel successful if he reaches his goal, even if it falls short of an external criterion. For example, the individual who is poor at English, and obtains a mark of 45 per cent, may feel well pleased with this 'failure' if his previous performance led him to believe a mark of over 35 per cent was an improvement. The assessment of achievement, therefore, is complex and cannot be determined purely by examining whether or not the individual has conformed to an external standard.

Locke's (1965) experiments did in fact examine the effect of the individual setting his own goals on job satisfaction. In one experiment a group was allowed to set its own standard for success. It was found that this group was more satisfied with the task than was a group with an equal degree of success but whose standard of success was set by the experimenters. The evidence on this point is far from convincing, however, and a study by Ivanecevich (1976) found achievement of imposed goals to be more satisfying than achievement of self-set goals for a group of sales personnel. He also found specific goals, whether imposed or self-set, were preferable to vague goals such as 'do your best'. The influence of different methods of goal-setting disappeared however, after a twelve-month period. Despite other studies, e.g. Arvey *et al.* (1976), this area needs more investigation.

Another factor which affects the extent to which the success or failure in a task influences satisfaction is the importance attached to the task by the individual. The worker inserting screws on a conveyor belt system has normally no significant challenge and no skill to apply, so that the job is hardly likely to be seen as important in relation to feelings of self-esteem.

Importance of the task can have two aspects: importance to the individual and importance to the organisation. For example, although it is vital to the army that soldiers shoot accurately, and whilst considerable skill is involved in accurate shooting, it may be the case that an individual soldier has an aversion to killing and therefore would regard his failure to shoot straight not as a failure but as a success. In considering the importance to the individual of the actual job being performed, Nord (1977) cites studies in which the workers were frustrated by the trivial nature of the products they were manufacturing.

The main point about success in relation to satisfaction is that it is success which is perceived of as being of significance to the individual – particularly, although not exclusively, in relation to self-esteem. Thus success in a difficult task is likely to increase self-esteem relative to success in an easy task. Success in a socially relevant situation is likely to give rise to feelings of approval from others and thus increase social prestige and feelings of self-esteem. Where enhanced self-esteem is possible, it is likely that the individual will come to identify with the task and become job involved and only if this happens is a relationship between satisfaction and success likely to occur.

Not only enhancing self-esteem, but carrying out a task which the individual enjoys entirely for its own sake is also important in the relationship between success and satisfaction. Thus an individual may regard a job as important in the wider social context, as requiring the application of skill and as one in which success is possible. Yet he may still find no job satisfaction. For example, I derive considerable satisfaction from teaching certain aspects of psychology. Were I required to teach other aspects, such as clinical psychology, to the exclusion of those aspects in which I am interested, I would become extremely job dissatisfied, even though the job would obviously still be an important one, requiring skill and having the potential for successful attainment in teaching and so on. The essential aspect is missing, that it is not the skill I want to exercise.

Not only can success be irrelevant to job satisfaction, satisfaction can be gained from activities in which one is regularly unsuccessful. Hoppock (1935), for example, cites the enjoyment derived by the duff golfer. In such cases, however, it could be argued that enjoyment is derived from the occasional successes, rather than from the frequent failures. Clearly, however, whilst task achievement is likely to have some relationship to job satisfaction, it is achievement in certain areas and under certain conditions only.

RECOGNITION

For many individuals, achievement sooner or later requires external validation (recognition) if it is to be sustained. For example, the researcher who has his research reports consistently rejected by editors of learned journals, rapidly becomes discouraged and his confidence (self-esteem) is likely to suffer. Without success in terms of having reports published in journals, most researchers would probably give up. Acceptance of material for publication, however, gives external validation of the worthwhile nature of a researcher's work and thus increases his feelings of self-esteem. It is also likely that acceptance of reports for publication will lead to further social rewards, such as increased status in the academic community, feelings of contributing to the advancement of a chosen discipline and so on. Thus, success produces a series of externally validated rewards, all of which have the effect of increasing the individual's self-esteem, where failure leads to a reduction in feelings of self-esteem.

In many industrial and commercial organisations, as well as in academic life, success is often externally signalled by promotion. Promotion does not universally signal recognition of achievement, however, as in some organisations promotion may result from seniority or length of stay in the organisation rather than from achievement on the job. Indeed, in certain occupations, such as in the Civil Service, promotion is often given as a result of success off the job, such as in external examinations. Nevertheless, in many cases, promotion within the organisation is the external recognition of a relatively successful job performance. Promotion, of course, has the other function of placing the most able people in the jobs which require the greatest exercise of skill. Promotion generally ceases when it is felt that the individual has reached his optimum level of competence.

The function of promotion will vary from organisation to organisation according to the relative importance placed on the two goals of recognition and the efficient utilisation of skills. Academic institutions in Britain, for example, promote lecturers to senior lecturers on the basis of past 'achievement' but do not expect any change in basic function from the promoted individual. In this case the function of promotion is clearly one of recognition. On the other hand, competitive industrial organisations must ensure that those promoted are those able to carry out more difficult decision-making so that reward for past services must take second place to the potential for making good decisions at a higher level.

A number of studies, however, have shown promotion as an external validation of recognition to be fraught with problems. First, there is the difficulty of making an objective assessment of an individual's worth. This is notoriously difficult, for example, in situations in which a superior must make a subjective report on a subordinate. Obvious difficulties involved in inter-personal relationships may colour judgements. Even 'objective' procedures, however, have their problems. Gruneberg, Startup and Tapsfield (1974a), for example, in a study of university teachers' satisfaction with promotion procedures, found promotion procedures to be the aspect of their job with which they were least satisfied, a finding confirmed in a study of American academics by Nicholson and Miljus (1972).

In the study by Gruneberg *et al.* (1974), only 20 per cent of senior lecturers were actually satisfied with the very promotion procedures from which they had benefited. The problem appears to be the weight placed on the number of publications when considering promotion, when other functions such as teaching and administration appear to be relatively ignored. Here the problem is how to give an objective assessment of teaching and administrative ability.

A second problem with promotion concerns the suggestion of inadequacy of those not promoted. It is quite probable, for example, that academics' complaints about the weight given to publications in promotion procedures are merely symptomatic of a basic dissatisfaction with a system in which some people are rewarded and others are not, when the difference in ability between them is difficult to determine. To promote some individuals and not others, in such a situation, is to imply that promoted individuals are somehow 'better' than the non-promoted individual in indeterminate ways, otherwise he too would have been promoted.

Of course, as far as the individual is concerned, promotion involves more than the recognition of achievement, it can also involve increases in financial reward and status. In this situation, however, salary cannot be regarded purely as a hygiene factor. It, too, is intimately related to status and recognition; the more one is financially rewarded, the greater is the recognition for services in an organisation. As Hoppock (1935) points out, money can act as an incentive because it affects the respect in which the individual is held by others. It is little wonder, therefore, that financial reward can sometimes be measured as a satisfier in job satisfaction.

As well as receiving recognition in tangible ways, such as through promotion and salary increases, recognition may be given by verbal comments, such as praise from one's supervisor for good work done. Locke (1976) argues that virtually all employees value being praised for their work by supervisors and colleagues. He found recognition to be one of the single most frequently cited events causing either satisfaction or dissatisfaction, and points out that those using Herzberg's theoretical framework frequently found recognition to be a major source of satisfaction.

Praise has the effect of increasing the self-esteem of the individual and also gives feedback as to how he is progressing. Feedback on job performance is, of course, essential if the individual is to have a chance of modifying his behaviour in the light of his past performance. If one does not know that one is screwing bolts too tight because no one is feeding this information back, any improvement in performance is impossible, so that the individual has no chance to develop his capacities and skills, which will lead in turn to recognition. There can be little doubt that employers wishing to improve the satisfaction of their employees must pay attention both to the feedback aspect of recognition and to the problems of recognition through formal procedures, such as promotion.

THE APPLICATION OF SKILL

Specialisation

In considering what is meant by 'achievement' in a job, it was noted that feelings of achievement depend on the individual perceiving the task as being important. This involved the application of some skill, in addition to the job having some wider significance for the individual.

The importance of various aspects of skill on job satisfaction was noted by Hoppock (1935) as being one of the principal areas of job satisfaction. Perhaps the study of Walker and Guest (1952), however, has been most influential in pointing out the relationship between skill level and job satisfaction.

Walker and Guest interviewed workers in an automobile plant in the United States. The plant used mass production methods in which the major aspect was the assembly line. Most of the jobs were therefore mechanically paced, rather than the individual having control over the speed at which he could work. In addition, the tasks were often repetitive in nature and limited in scope, thus denying the possibility of applying any real skill to the job. The tasks also had a further undesirable consequence in limiting social interaction, since the individual had to stay in the same place and concentrate exclusively on a small number of mechanically paced tasks. Typical of the type of job is that of a seat-spring builder:

> I work on a small conveyor which goes round in a circle. We call it a merry-go-round. I make up zig-zag springs for front seats. Every couple of feet on the conveyor there is a form for the pieces that make up the seat springs. As that form goes by

me, I clip several pieces together, using a clip gun. I then put the pieces back on the form, and it goes on around to where other men clip more pieces together. By the time the form has gone round the whole line, the pieces are ready to be set in a frame where they are made into a complete seat spring. That's further down the main seat cushion line. The only operation I do is work the clip gun. It takes just a couple of seconds to shoot six or eight clips onto the spring and I do it as I walk a few steps. Then I start right over again.

As Walker and Guest note, the job is paced by a moving conveyor, lacks variety and has little skill requirement.

Nevertheless, even on the assembly line, not all the jobs were alike either in skill, variety or the degree of satisfaction obtained. Walker and Guest, for example, quote the job description of a utility man; where the application of skill is required and where there was considerable job variety.

I work the whole length of that part of the chassis line beginning with motor drop up to where the wheels are mounted. My job is to fill in wherever I am needed. A man might be absent or away from the job or may need help on the job.

We start where the motor is lowered onto the frame (motor mount). The clutch assembly is installed and hooked up. Then the exhaust system is attached and the bolts tightened. The clutch assembly bolts are also tightened. In the next area on the line the brake chambers are filled and bled.

Off to the side, the subassembly men put the steering column together. The steering post and the Pittman arm assembly are put in. Further down the line, men put in air cleaners and inject hydraulic fluid for the transmission.

Next, the brakes are tested and the clutch linkage hooked up. The bumper brackets are put on; a serial number is attached next; and then the bumper brackets are tightened up. Finally, the chassis is sprayed, mounted on wheels, and moved on toward the body drop. All in all, about 28 men work on these jobs, each man with his own special operation. I go on each of these jobs, depending on where I am needed most. It is different each day. Some of the jobs are hard to learn, so when I take over one on which I haven't had much experience, it's hard to keep up. I have been learning how to do the work ever since I've been in the plant. I can never learn everything because new changes are always being made.

Walker and Guest examined the relationship between the number of operations performed and the degree of satisfaction, and found that the number of operations alone discriminated between those satisfied and those dissatisfied with their jobs. For example, for those with one operation to perform, nineteen found the job interesting and thirty-eight did not find it interesting. For those with five or more operations to perform, forty-one found the job interesting and only eighteen did not find it interesting. The repetitive nature of the job was given by the majority of workers as a criticism of the job, thus confirming the impression given by the figures.

As Walker and Guest point out, however, not everyone dislikes the repetitiveness of his job. They could find no way in which those satisfied differed from those dissatisfied.

Apart from the study of Walker and Guest, the positive relationship between the use of skills and job satisfaction has been reported as statistically significant in a considerable number of studies. Vroom (1962), for example, found a high correlation (0.59) between opportunity for self-expression and job satisfaction. Opportunity for self-expression was determined by answers to questions such as: 'How much chance is there to use the skills you have learned on the job?' Similarly, since Walker and Guest, a number of studies have shown a relationship between job satisfaction and degree of specialisation. Mann and Hoffman (1960), for example, found that job satisfaction increased when workers in one plant were transferred to another which required a greater number of duties.

Despite such findings, some investigators such as Sexton (1968) argue that there is no need to suppose that highly structured work is necessarily psychologically 'devastating'. One argument that Sexton puts forward is that highly routine jobs allow the individual to 'switch off', to day-dream and to think about other aspects of his life which are significant to him. Jobs with somewhat greater variety may still have no significance to the individual but require a degree of concentration which does not allow him to 'switch off'. This may be the reason why, for example, routine clerical jobs are so dissatisfying for so many people. It must be pointed out that Sexton produces no evidence that this 'switching off' takes place to a significant extent.

Recently, an influential study by Hackman and Lawler (1971) has clarified the relationship between job characteristics and job satisfaction. The study examined the job attitudes of employees at a telephone company, in relation to what Hackman and Lawler describe as four core element of a job, namely, job variety, job autonomy, job identity and feedback. The question of feedback has been discussed previously, the other three aspects will be considered in turn.

Job variety

As far as job variety (task specialisation) is concerned, Hackman and Lawler confirmed the findings of Walker and Guest in showing a relationship between the variety in a job and job satisfaction. The correlation between general job satisfaction and task variety was 0·38. For specific aspects of job satisfaction, such as self-esteem obtained from the job, feelings of personal growth, and satisfaction with prestige of the job, the correlation with task variety was never less than 0·30. Thus it seems fair to conclude with Walker and Guest that jobs which have little variety, on average lead to lower job satisfaction.

In their study, Walker and Guest noted that some individuals were happy with jobs which offered little variety but were unable to find a means of distinguishing such individuals from those who were dissatisfied with repetitive jobs. Hackman and Lawler examined this problem by looking at the expressed higher order needs of individuals, such as the desired opportunity for personal growth, and the opportunity to do challenging work. They found, perhaps not surprisingly, that those who did not feel a great need to have an opportunity for growth or to do challenging work were less dissatisfied with jobs offering little variety. For example, the correlation between satisfaction and task variety for those with strong higher order needs was 0·41 and for those with weak higher order needs the correlation was only 0·28. More telling, perhaps, were the relationships between the extent of specific needs and task variety. For those with strong higher order needs, the correlation between satisfaction with personal growth and task variety was 0·55, for those with weak higher order needs it was 0·33. Given that a repetitive job can hardly offer possibilities for personal growth, this difference between those with and without higher order needs is, to say the least, not surprising. Nevertheless, it does reinforce what writers such as Sexton have argued, that it is not merely the characteristics of the job which determine whether variety will lead to satisfaction. One must take into account what the person wants from his job. Those without higher order needs will not necessarily be dissatisfied with jobs lacking in variety.

Differences in individual need are not the only important factor in determining whether or not a job of a particular skill level will lead to satisfaction. The matching of individual abilities to skill level is important. It has often been hypothesised that those with too much ability will be dissatisfied with a job at a particular level just as much as those with too little ability. Vroom (1964), for example, cites a study in which it was found that the more intelligent clerical workers tended to leave the easier jobs and stay in the more difficult ones, whereas for the less intelligent, the reverse was the case. One factor which may affect the relationship between intelligence and job satisfaction is role overload and role underload, where giving an individual too much or too little to do in terms of his capacities causes frustration and job stress.

Job autonomy

In relation to job satisfaction, Hackman and Lawler (1971) define autonomy in terms of the employee having a major say in scheduling his work, selecting the equipment to be used and deciding on procedures to be adopted. In terms of its importance to satisfaction, it appears that what is true for task variety is also true for task autonomy. Thus the overall correlation between job satisfaction and degree of autonomy was 0·39. Again there were differences between those with strong higher order needs and those with low higher order needs, the correlation between job satisfaction and autonomy being 0·43 and 0·29, for those with higher and lower order needs, respectively.

The degree to which one has freedom to make decisions about one's job does, of course, determine the amount of skill which one can apply. Even if one has a job with 100 operations, if the order of these operations and the way in which they should be carried out is determined by someone else, then there is a considerable reduction in the skill required in the exercise of the job. Only a job which allows the individual to apply a skill can reasonably be expected to allow possibilities for growth in self-esteem due to successful completion of the task. If the skill aspect is removed then successful performance is someone else's success. As Hackman and Lawler point out, however, this does not necessarily mean that group projects cannot lead to feelings of success, simply that the individual must be able to feel that he has had some responsibility for the group success. Responsibility for making decisions concerning one's job is therefore a prerequisite of applying a skill, so it is hardly surprising that those with a high need for personal growth are more satisfied when they are given responsibility to determine their own work methods.

In view of this, it is not difficult to see why Walker and Guest's study revealed dissatisfaction with the mechanical pacing of the conveyor belt. It removes from the individual the possibility of making decisions for himself regarding the order of operations and the speed at which operations can take place. In so doing, the job removes the possibility of applying the individual's own skills.

Of course, as Vroom points out, it is not only mechanical pacing, but in many cases, human interference by one's supervisor which reduces the possibility of exercising skill. A supervisor, for example, may lay down very strict instructions covering how a particular piece of work should be conducted.

One final finding of Hackman and Lawler, in relation to autonomy, deserves comment. They found a very strong relationship between task variety and job autonomy. This suggested to the investigators that as both factors enhanced the meaningfulness of the job, it might not be necessary to measure both. Yet whilst it is obvious that one cannot have much freedom of choice concerning how to do a job if there is only one operation to perform, it is equally obvious that situations might arise in which there are a large number of operations to be performed, but that the method of performing them is strictly laid down by the superior. The strong relationship found in the study of Hackman and Lawler, therefore, will not necessarily be found in other studies. Indeed, in view of the discussion on clerical work earlier, it might be that increasing job variety without increasing autonomy could lead to increased dissatisfaction. In such a case, the individual has a reduced chance of escaping from the job into activities such as day-dreaming.

Task identity

A third core aspect of the job which Hackman and Lawler relate to job satisfaction is task identity. As was noted earlier, even where a job enables the individual to perform successfully, this is unlikely to lead to job satisfaction unless the job has significance for him as an individual. As Hackman and Lawler note, however, it is impossible to make any generalisations about what makes individuals interested in particular jobs, as people differ too much in the things which they value. Hackman and Lawler argue that a 'job characteristic which will enable those with higher order needs to achieve satisfaction is that the task should be a sufficiently whole piece of work so that the individual can see that he has produced something worthwhile'. In their study of telephone operators, Hackman and Lawler show a significant relationship between 'wholeness' of the work (task identity) and job satisfaction. Of course, it is possible for some jobs to be 'whole' yet to be small scale, and, therefore, relate little to job satisfaction. For example, Hackman and Lawler's telephone operators handled calls and thus dealt with a 'whole' job, but it was frequently repeated in the course of the day. It would appear, therefore, that task identity only has relevance for job satisfaction when the job is sufficiently large scale to allow the worker to utilise skills in carrying out the job. Otherwise the job is unlikely to be meaningful to the individual and hence to involve him in it.*

JOB INVOLVEMENT

It was noted earlier that the potential for application of skill, the social significance of the job and even success are not enough to ensure job satisfaction. Job satisfaction involves the exercise of a particular skill which the individual sees as having some significance to himself, so that he can identify with it. The extent to which the individual identifies with the job is known as job involvement.

There is little doubt that job involvement is a major aspect of job satisfaction, although the two terms are by no means synonymous. It is quite conceivable, for example, for a person to be very involved with his job and yet be very frustrated because it is not going well. It seems reasonable to conclude that the greater the job involvement, the greater will be either job satisfaction or job dissatisfaction. Job involvement, in other words, is necessary

---

* In a later paper Hackman *et al.* (1975) do in fact add task significance as a further core aspect of the job. By this they mean the degree to which the job has a substantial and perceptible impact on the lives of others. The person tightening bolts on an aircraft, for example, is more likely to see his work as significant than the man filling boxes of paper clips, even if the level of skill is identical. Hackman *et al.* argue that task significance is an important aspect of job satisfaction (see Chapter 7).

if there is to be any possibility of deriving satisfaction from a job (as opposed to being satisfied with a job), but it by no means guarantees satisfaction. Despite this, a number of studies have been reported which have shown a relationship between job satisfaction and job involvement. For example, Lodahl and Kejner (1965), in a study of engineers, found high job involvement to be related to satisfaction with the work itself, and to satisfaction with supervisors, promotion and interaction with people.

A study by Weissenberg and Gruenfeld (1968) throws further light on the relationship between satisfaction and job involvement. They used Herzberg's dichotomy between motivators and hygiene factors and found job involvement to be related to three motivator variables (recognition, achievement and responsibility), and one hygiene factor (personal relationships). Strangely, perhaps, they found no relationship between job involvement and satisfaction with the work itself.

At least one further study, that of Hall, Schneider and Nygren (1970), supports Weissenberg and Gruenfeld's view that job involvement is related to motivators rather than hygiene factors. The distinction between motivators and hygiene factors in the context of job involvement is interesting in that it tends to support Herzberg's view of the separability of the two sets of factors. Thus whilst one can be satisfied with a job in which one is not involved, perhaps because the pay is good, one cannot derive satisfaction from the job unless one is involved. Other studies reviewed by Rabinowitz and Hall (1977), lead to the conclusion that the results obtained by Weissenberg and Gruenfeld are typical, to the extent that they show a relationship between job involvement and some aspects of job satisfaction.

What factors, then, influence job involvement? Psychologists have taken two distinct approaches to the problem. Some, such as Lodhal (1964), regard job involvement as a basic characteristic of the individual. Some individuals will become job involved, almost irrespective of the work situation, whereas others will not. Lodahl, for example, argues that the orientation towards work is learned early in the process of growing up. Attitudes to work are absorbed from parents, friends and the general sub-culture in which the individual lives. For some individuals this will involve taking on the so-called 'protestant' work ethic, which involves the belief that hard work is morally good.

The notion that attitudes to work are grounded in the individual at a relatively early age is supported by the work of Hulin and Blood (1968), who found that many blue collar workers in urban as opposed to rural areas did not seek to derive satisfaction from the nature of the work they were doing. They regarded their jobs purely as a means to an end, so that they could satisfy 'off the job' interests. Given the narrow nature of the jobs in which they were placed, such job attitudes, as was noted previously, might reasonably be regarded as healthy. Again, if children in a particular area have no expectations other than the dull routine jobs in which their fathers are employed, it is not surprising that work attitudes prior to taking a job are negative. Research suggests, however, that such negative attitudes on the part of individuals are amenable to change, provided the expectations that people can have about employment are changed.

In contrast to the view that an individual will or will not become job involved according to his upbringing and background, is the view that job involvement is determined by the actual situation in which an individual finds himself. Theorists such as Argyris (1964) argue that the organisational structure precludes the possibility of the individual being involved in the job. In particular, job specialisation and deskilling give no opportunities to identify with a job as a meaningful aspect of one's life.

As with most aspects of behaviour, it is likely that job involvement encompasses characteristics of both the individual and the situation. Few people, however much they adhere to the protestant ethic, could become involved with a conveyor belt job and, fortunately for most middle-class individuals, they are rarely faced with the situation. On the other hand, there are individuals who, because of their upbringing and attitude to work, are unlikely to identify with jobs which allow for personal growth and development. It therefore seems useful to look at both individual characteristics and the organisational situation when examining job involvement.

As far as individual characteristics are concerned, Rabinowitz and Hall (1977) have examined the relationship between job involvement and variables such as sex, age, education, length of service and marital status. For all these variables, the relationship with job involvement was either very low or the evidence was contradictory. Rabinowitz and Hall's review of job involvement and ageing, for example, found the evidence to be mixed, with some studies finding job involvement to increase with age, and other studies showing no such relationship. A major methodological problem is that people with low job involvement will tend to leave their employment until they can find a job with which they can become job involved. The older the individual, the more chance he will have had to do this. The same problems arise with length of service, although here again, the evidence is by no means unanimous. From the point of view of selecting individuals who are likely to be job involved, therefore, individual factors such as age and sex offer relatively little.

On the other hand, one individual factor which does seem to be significantly related to job involvement is strength of higher order needs. When comparing those with higher and those with lower order needs, Hackman and Lawler found significant differences in the correlation between job involvement and core aspects of the job. The correlations reported were 0·45 for those with higher order needs and 0·28 for those with lower order needs. Thus, the results indicate that workers with higher order needs were more likely to become involved in jobs which gave the opportunity for satisfying higher order needs.

With respect to the effect of situational factors on job involvement, Rabinowitz and Hall examined such factors as decision-making, social aspects and job characteristics. In examining participation in decision-making, the reviewers noted a number of studies which showed reasonably high correlations (about 0·5) with job involvement. Similarly, social factors such as whether individuals are part of a team or working alone have also been found to relate significantly to job involvement. Other situational factors which have been shown to relate to job involvement are achievement and responsibility.

On the basis of the evidence it seems fair to conclude that both situational and personality factors can affect job involvement. There is, however, a major difficulty which deserves comment. Almost all of the studies deal with people once they have chosen a particular job or occupation and they may, therefore, have some intrinsic job involvement to begin with. Findings concerning an increase in job involvement for engineers following a job redesign, for example, may have no implications for arousing the interest of non-engineers in engineering, however skilled and socially relevant the job is.

This is not merely an academic point since, as has been noted above, the essence of job satisfaction is not the exercise of a skill *per se*, or the success or social significance of a job. The essence of job satisfaction is surely being able to exercise the skill of one's choice and no amount of correlational evidence on the relationship between job characteristics and job involvement throws light on how an individual can come to develop an interest in a particular skill which was previously absent. As Rabinowitz and Hall conclude:

> Since most of our work has been static research, we know very little about the process of becoming involved in a job. Future longitudinal research should do more than correlate changes in predicator variables with changes in involvement. Methods are needed that will reveal the sequence of events and processes that take place as a person becomes 'turned on' to his or her work.

For practical purposes, of course, the critical point is to select for a job an individual whose job involvement and practical skill are in the area of that job. Among the items given by Rabinowitz and Hall, as a tentative profile for identifying those job involved are:

1. A belief in the 'protestant' ethic.
2. The older age group (the older the employee the greater the job involvement).
3. Internal locus of control.
4. Strong growth needs.
5. Having a stimulating job (high autonomy, variety, task identity and feedback).
6. Having a job which allows participation in decisions.
7. Satisfaction with the job.
8. A history of success.

Having selected the right man, it then is a question of whether organisational variables will suppress job involvement or allow them to develop. It must be stressed again, however, that little is known about how an individual who is not previously involved in a particular job 'takes' to a new job situation. The check-list suggested by Rabinowitz and Hall must not, therefore, be given too much weight.

Job involvement, then, is an essential aspect of job satisfaction and studies have shown a correlation between the two. Job involvement is likely to increase either satisfaction or dissatisfaction with the job. Both individual factors, including personality, and factors on the job affect job involvement. Among the most important factors appear to be the individual's need to have a challenging job, and a job which allows for the application of skill, responsibility and the possibility of individual achievement.

SUMMARY AND CONCLUSIONS

This chapter has looked at various factors affecting the individual's satisfaction with the actual job performed. The first of these, success or achievement, has been shown to be related to liking for the job, presumably because success enhances an individual's self-esteem. On the other hand, success must be in something significant to the individual and must involve the application of some skill.

In many cases, the question of whether performance will be considered successful depends not only on whether the individual feels that he has been successful but whether others accord the individual recognition for his achievements. This recognition might be intangible, in the form of the supervisor offering praise, or tangible, in the form of promotion and possibly a higher salary. It can be seen, therefore, that financial reward may not simply be a hygiene factor in Herzberg's terms, but may also be an indication of the esteem in which the person is held within the organisation.

Whatever the nature of external recognition, the individual is unlikely to feel that he has achieved something worthwhile unless the application of some skill is involved. A number of studies have shown that jobs which are deskilled and lack variety and autonomy are less satisfying than are jobs which allow for the individual's abilities to emerge. In addition, jobs which have no clear beginning, middle and end (task identity) have little meaning for most individuals. The evidence overwhelmingly suggests that such deskilled jobs allow for less satisfaction than do jobs which allow for development and growth. This is despite the undoubted fact that, for some individuals, deskilled jobs are not dissatisfying. Such individuals appear to have no wish to have higher order needs satisfied on the job. On the other hand, the work of Walker and Guest (1952) and of Kornhauser (1965) showed that between a quarter and a half of those on an automobile production line had mental health problems in connection with their jobs, surely showing that deskilling a job has a major effect on job satisfaction for a large number of people. One reason why the application of a skill is necessary for job satisfaction is that it allows the individual a certain amount of freedom and responsibility in his job. Job operations, however, do not require skill if they are predetermined by a supervisor and by machinery.

A major aspect of whether or not a job is meaningful for an individual is the extent to which he becomes involved in the job. Job involvement implies an identification with the job so that success or failure is related back to the individual. This aspect of a job is critical for job satisfaction, as the application of a skill and success does not determine job satisfaction, unless the skill and success are something which the individual regards as important. Nevertheless, many of the factors discussed above, such as achievement and the possibility of using one's own skills, do relate to the degree of job involvement.

The characteristics of the job itself, then, are clearly the major factor in determining whether or not satisfaction will be derived from a job. This view is shared by practically all present-day organisational psychologists, whatever their theoretical orientation, and has led many to agree with Herzberg that any improvement in job satisfaction depends on redesigning jobs so that personal growth and development is possible. Yet satisfaction with the job itself is not the be-all and end-all of job satisfaction. It is interesting to note that the great majority of Hoppock's least satisfied teachers found the job itself interesting. Other factors, such as pay, social interactions and supervision all have a significant effect on the individual's feeling of wellbeing on the job. These are considered in the next chapter.

4 Job Satisfaction and Context Factors

In the last chapter, it was seen how critical was the nature of the job itself in determining whether the individual was satisfied or not with his job. As noted previously, factors associated with the job itself have been described as intrinsic or content factors, whilst those such as pay, supervision, etc. have been described as extrinsic or context factors. This distinction corresponds roughly to Herzberg's distinction between motivators and hygiene factors. Whilst most recent work has concentrated on the importance of content aspects of job satisfaction, few workers deny the importance of context factors. Even Herzberg regards factors such as pay as of critical importance, since deficiencies in pay may prevent the individual from concentrating on those aspects of the job which are potentially fulfilling. Other workers, such as Locke (1976), regard extrinsic factors in a somewhat different light. They consider both kinds of factor as being capable of causing both satisfaction and dissatisfaction, but generally regard context factors as less important to job satisfaction than content factors. Nevertheless, few would deny that the former are of considerable importance, and in this chapter the main context factors are considered. The factors are (1) Pay, (2) Security, (3) Work-Groups, (4) Supervision, (5) Participation, (6) Role Conflict and Ambiguity, and (7) Organisation Structure and Organisational Climate.

1 SATISFACTION WITH PAY

The importance of money

It is self-evident that satisfaction with pay is an important element in our job satisfaction. Few, if any of us, would work in our present employment if our pay was seen to be totally inadequate. Yet the evidence relating to the importance of pay in job satisfaction is surprisingly conflicting, with some studies apparently showing that pay is of little importance in relation to one's job satisfaction. For example, Opsahl and Dunnette (1966) cite a study in which about 42 000 individuals were asked to rank ten job factors in order of importance. Pay came sixth. On the other hand, they also cite a study of English skilled and semi-skilled workers in which pay was shown to be the most important job factor. Reviewing the literature, Lawler (1971) found pay to be reported as the job aspect with which the greatest number of employees expressed dissatisfaction although on average pay was rated third in importance. This is unfortunately a somewhat meaningless average for at least three reasons. Firstly, there are, as noted above, major discrepancies between studies, which may reflect the different attitudes of different groups of people towards the importance of pay. For example, in jobs which give little prospect of utilising skill, it might be expected that individuals would place more emphasis on money. Secondly, discrepancies between studies might occur because different studies use different lists of job factors and ask different questions of their respondents. Thirdly, as Lawler points out, most of the research is poorly designed, so that any conclusions drawn from them must be regarded with suspicion.

In assessing the research findings, an important consideration is that whatever people say, they do behave as if they think money is of great importance. Opsahl and Dunnette point out that executives strive to reach higher paid jobs, entertainers work for more lucrative arrangements, bankers embezzle, robbers rob and university teachers publish to increase their earnings. Money seems to be so central to our thinking in relation to our jobs that it leads one to be suspicious about research findings which report money as being of relatively low importance. The reason for the difference between actual and reported importance of money might well be due to people distorting their replies to questionnaires. It may well be for example that many individuals do not think it 'proper' to admit that their main motivation for working is financial, rather than for the intrinsic interest of the job itself. Indeed, if one were being interviewed for a job, it would be foolish to admit that money, rather than the job itself, was of highest importance. This might well explain why, in one of the studies cited by Opsahl and Dunnette, pay was reported as sixth in importance. The 42000 individuals studied were *applicants* for jobs with the Minneapolis Gas Company. Whilst the potential for distortion might not be so great in other studies, the possibility of socially desirable responses distorting the true picture of the importance of money has to be borne in mind.

The meaning of money

One difficulty in assessing the importance of money for job satisfaction is that it means much more than just the amount of goods and services that can be bought with it. For example, as noted previously, the amount of money which one receives is sometimes an indication of one's value to an organisation, so it is associated with achievement and recognition by one's peers. It is extremely difficult, therefore, to test adequately Herzberg's contention that money is a hygiene factor, because it can take on symbolic functions of indicating recognition and achievement.

The question of what money means to individuals has been examined by Wernimont and Fitzpatrick (1972) who examined groups such as trainees, employees and students. They confirmed the view that money has a great deal of symbolic value, but that the nature of this value varies with the background of the individuals concerned. For example, money is regarded as a 'good' thing by those in employment, whereas students place little value on money as a 'good thing'. Wernimont and Fitzpatrick suggest that this might reflect a generation gap, but another possible explanation is in terms of 'sour grapes'. If you lack something which is desirable, you devalue its significance in order to maintain your self-esteem. Again, as Wernimont and Fitzpatrick point out, there are large differences in the meaning of money according to one's stage of development and one's experiences, sex, economic status and personality. For example, a person well-off from birth is unlikely to associate money with hardship and unhappiness in the way than many unemployed individuals do.

Money, then, has different meanings for different individuals and can act as an indicator of recognition and achievement. This should not detract, however, from the potentially important effect of money on satisfaction that can arise from increasing material wellbeing. As will be seen in Chapter 6, job and life satisfaction tend to be related and where a job produces financial rewards such that one can satisfy the material wants of one's family, it is likely to reflect back on feelings regarding the job. This, of course, can also have a negative aspect in that poor pay is likely to be associated with poor home conditions which will reflect negatively on the job. This may happen through wives complaining of the low level of material satisfaction, blaming the husband for lack of job success and thus reducing his level of self-esteem. For those outside the job, perhaps more than for those inside, money can be seen as an objective measure of job success.

Factors associated with pay satisfaction

Of central importance to an understanding of satisfaction with pay is the question of what factors are associated with pay satisfaction. Lawler (1971), after examining the literature, concluded that factors such as education, skill, job performance, age, seniority, sex, organisational level, time-span, non-monetary outcomes, amount of pay and payments method were all associated with satisfaction with pay. Schwab and Wallace (1974), however, note the inadequacy of many of the studies examined.

Nevertheless, some variables, such as actual level of pay, do seem to be clearly related, not surprisingly, to satisfaction with pay. However, it is not necessarily actual level of pay which is related to job satisfaction, but relative levels, that is, the amount of pay received relative to others with whom one is comparing oneself. Support for this view comes from the work of equity theorists, discussed in Chapter 2. As Warr and Wall (1975) point out, this is hardly surprising for anyone engaged in wages bargaining. Where other comparable groups receive a wages increase, your own group wants an increase.

Another variable shown by Schwab and Wallace to be related to satisfaction with pay is position in the organisation. When controlling for actual pay, it appears that the higher up one is in the organisation, the less is one satisfied with pay. One probable explanation for this is the finding reported by Lawler that managers over-estimate the amount of pay received by their subordinates. This happens, in fact, because of the secrecy surrounding the payment that individuals actually receive. Given the probability that pay satisfaction depends to some extent on a comparison with what others are getting, an over-assessment of what others below you are getting is likely to lead to dissatisfaction.

Of the other variables examined by Schwab and Wallace, sex was related to pay satisfaction in that females were more satisfied with pay than were males. Perhaps females have fewer expectations regarding pay, perhaps in this particular study they regarded themselves as relatively better off than women workers elsewhere. As will be seen in Chapter 5, sex differences in job satisfaction are so erratic that not too much can be made of findings showing significant differences in any one study. Schwab and Wallace found no relationship between age and satisfaction in their study, contrary to findings of studies reviewed by Lawler. Here again, however, results are often inconsistent (see Chapter 5).

Payment systems

There is one major dispute between the work of Lawler and

Schwab and Wallace, and this covers the important issue of payment systems. Lawler argues that incentive schemes (where individuals are paid for output) are more satisfying than schemes involving hourly work. Schwab and Wallace (1974), on the other hand, found hourly workers to be more satisfied with their method of payment than those on piece-work and they cite three studies which support their view. Again, Opsahl and Dunnette (1966) cite a number of studies in which preference was expressed for straight salary payments rather than incentive payments. Furthermore, studies of some group incentive schemes show them to be unpopular with the majority of workers, although results are inconsistent and, in one study at least, over 60 per cent of workers expressed approval for a group incentive scheme (Warr and Wall, 1975).

It appears likely, therefore, that hourly payment systems are more popular than piece-work systems. The reason for this, suggested by Schwab and Wallace, is that piece-work systems are disruptive of social relationships and other satisfactions to be obtained from work. Furthermore, they are often disruptive in that they set one worker against another. Again, however, because satisfaction with one's own pay appears to depend substantially on what other people are getting, difficulties arise in establishing comparability between groups on what is equitable to produce and receive for different methods of operation.

Given that hourly paid schemes may be more popular than incentive schemes, the question arises as to whether there are differences in satisfaction with different kinds of incentive schemes. Comparisons between the two suggest that individual incentive schemes are preferable to group schemes. The reason for this is not difficult to see. In individual incentive schemes the individual can relate his own individual effort directly to performance and monetary reward. In group schemes, the individual is dependent, not only on his own effort, but on that of others with whom he is working. He may, therefore, feel dissatisfaction in situations where he feels others are not pulling their weight. Unfortunately, in many jobs, individual incentive schemes are not directly applicable, as cooperation amongst group members might be essential, rather than the individual maximising his own productivity. When considering incentive schemes, therefore, it would seem desirable to limit the number in a group as far as possible since the fewer involved, the more directly is effort related to reward.

As Opsahl and Dunnette point out, satisfaction with pay is not necessarily related to productivity. Just because individuals feel happier with hourly pay does not mean that this gives rise to the greatest amount of productivity. On the contrary, as Warr and Wall note, incentive schemes normally result in increased productivity. They therefore suggest the value of a three-tier system of payment which (a) takes account of the individual's desire for a basic salary, but (b) includes an element of individual or group incentive, and (c) adds on a percentage for profitability of the organisation as a whole. In terms of a pay-packet, they suggest the three elements might contribute 70 per cent, 25 per cent and 5 per cent respectively. Such a scheme, argue Warr and Wall, is likely to be popular with blue collar workers but much less so with white collar workers where productivity is far more difficult to measure and agree on.

The causes of pay satisfaction

Finally, the question has to be asked: what causes pay satisfaction? One important factor noted above was the comparison that individuals make between themselves and others. As was noted in Chapter 2, however, this is at best only a partial explanation of job satisfaction because we do not know how people choose those with whom they compare themselves in terms of inputs as well as outputs. Presumably, such factors as level of skill, amount of effort, responsibility and past experience are some of the considerations which an individual weighs up on the input side. The equity of payment for this input is related to the amount of pay that similar individuals receive for similar inputs. There are, however, likely to be other factors affecting satisfaction with pay, such as level of aspirations. Thus an individual may be dissatisfied because his pay does not enable him to acquire the kind of material goods society has to offer. He may be dissatisfied because the level of pay received is insufficient to avert domestic conflict over the acquisition of material goods, and he may be dissatisfied in relation to the amount he is presently receiving compared to what he received one, two or five years ago. So complex is the problem, that Dyer and Theriault (1976) advise that their findings 'seem to support the apparent futility of searching for a universal determinant of pay satisfaction'.

Summary

It is quite clear that pay is an essential aspect of job satisfaction, despite self report surveys which sometimes place pay as being of low importance to overall job satisfaction. Pay means more to individuals than just the potential of acquiring material goods. It can be an indication of achievement and recognition or, conversely, of failure. It appears that money means different things to different groups, and is likely to have greater importance for individuals who cannot gain other satisfactions from their job.

Among the variables that are regarded as being related to satisfaction with pay are level of actual pay, position in the organisation, sex and payments systems. The latter is of considerable importance although the evidence is subject to some dispute. However, it appears that hourly paid work is preferred to piecework payment as the latter induces friction and conflict and disrupts social groups. On the other hand, it does appear that piece-rate working normally increases productivity if not satisfaction. Individual incentive schemes appear to be preferred to group incentive schemes, although in many situations individual incentive schemes may not be appropriate.

As to the causes of satisfaction with pay, many investigators regard an important aspect to be the comparison process between what an individual puts into a job and gets out of it in relation to what other people put into a job and get out of it. So complex is this process, however, that we are far from understanding what is involved in satisfaction with pay.

2 SECURITY

In many ways the question of security is more fundamental to job satisfaction than any other aspect of a job. Whatever the defects of the actual job being carried out, whatever the defects of pay and conditions, the major dichotomy in our society is between those with a job and those without. Being without a job carries implications, however unjust, of individual incompetence and lack of worth. A number of studies, for example, Siassi, Crocetti and Spiro (1975), have shown a greater incidence of mental ill health in the unemployed, and although this might be interpreted to indicate that those with mental health problems find it difficult to get jobs, it does appear likely that the value placed on work in our society leads to depression in those who cannot find work.

Being unemployed, of course, means more than a failure to find fulfilment in work; it also means that the level of personal well-being is at a minimum and status and prestige within our society is low. Little wonder that job security is a high priority for those whose job is threatened. One study, for example (Mann and Williams, 1962), found that job restructuring led to greater satisfaction with the job itself, with responsibility, and with the opportunity to develop. Yet overall job satisfaction did not increase because the restructuring of the job led to greater insecurity and fear of losing jobs.

Security is, of course, a classic example of a hygiene factor, paramount when it is absent and causing dissatisfaction, but apparently unimportant when there is no threat to the job. Here, however, is an example where a critical incident technique would bias findings, in that feeling good about the fact that one's job is secure is a background factor that is perhaps continually contributing to job satisfaction. There are perhaps more likely to be actual incidents concerning security where it is a problem.

3 JOB SATISFACTION AND WORK-GROUPS

The importance of the work-group

As with pay, the importance of co-workers figures prominently as a factor in studies of job satisfaction. Herzberg *et al.* (1957), in their review of the literature, found that social aspects of the job were rated first, on average, in response to the question of what made people most satisfied or dissatisfied with their job. Bearing in mind the limitations noted previously of rating facets of jobs, it seems self-evident that social interactions at work are likely to provide a major source of satisfaction. It is, after all, through our personal relationships, such as those with family and friends, that we give and receive most of life's pleasures. The work situation is merely an extension of our social interactions. Moreover, we are likely to interact with others to a greater extent 'on the job' than with many other 'off the job' friends and even close family!

The need for social interaction with others is one of the basic lower order needs put forward by Maslow, and there are a number of studies showing the domoralising effects of social isolation in work situations. Walker and Guest, for example, showed that individuals isolated from others because of the design of the job, tended to be more dissatisfied with their jobs than others. Furthermore, a study by Van Zelst (1952) shows that where individuals are allowed to increase the social satisfaction they derive from their work, this increases job satisfaction. On the basis of individuals' choices of work-mates, groups of workers were constituted to work together. The workers' skill and personalities were all previously known to each other. It was found that when the individuals were allowed to choose their own work-mates, then job satisfaction as well as turnover and costs all improved significantly. Whilst not conclusive, the study strongly suggests the importance of social interaction in improving job satisfaction. An alternative possibility is that by allowing individuals to choose their work-mates, people come to work in groups with roughly equal levels of skill and performance. Individuals are thus able to work compatibly at their own pace. Certainly the findings of Cross and Warr (1971) indicate that where work-groups are constituted in terms of similar levels of skill of individuals, satisfaction and productivity increase.

A study by Trist and Bamforth (1951) indicates clearly the demoralising effects of disrupting ongoing social interactions. Their study involved examining the effects of introducing new technology into coal-mines in Britain. Until the time at which the new machinery was introduced, coal working was carried out by small, tightly knit work-groups who knew each other and chose each other. An important aspect of mining communities is that social relationships outside the work situation are also extremely strong, reinforcing the social satisfaction derived from the work situation. The new 'longwall' system of coal-mining involved a re-organisation of work-groups so that instead of small groups of between two and eight men, working on all aspects of coal extraction, groups of up to fifty men, each with specialist tasks, were introduced. One important effect of the change was that communication between individuals was considerably curtailed because of the increased physical distance between men made necessary by the new system.

Predictably, the introduction of the new method of mining had bad effects. Absence, conflict and psychosomatic illness increased markedly, and production failed to live up to expectations. Job satisfaction fell and the generally unfavourable response to the new system forced management to change the method of work organisation. In particular, task specialisation and work relationships were altered with the result that morale improved.

Studies such as those of Van Zelst, and Trist and Bamforth, show clearly the important psychological effects of supportive work-groups. The study of Van Zelst, of course, also shows that we do not get equal amounts of satisfaction from interacting with other individuals, in all situations, only when workers chose their work-mates did satisfaction improve. It is clear that we derive satisfaction only from certain kinds of social interaction in certain kinds of situation. Miners, for example, are often in conditions of danger and stress and, like soldiers in time of war, are probably in a situation which encourages the depth of social relationships which is found among them.

Studies such as those of Trist and Bamforth have led to the view that jobs should be designed to take account both of the technology and the social systems involved. Where possible, technology should be modified to take account of the fact that individuals have social needs which, if ignored, may result in under-utilisation of the technology, as occured in the Trist and Bamforth study.

Group attractiveness

What affects the attractiveness of groups as far as individuals are concerned, has formed the subject of considerable study by psychologists. Clearly physical closeness is important, since if people are not close to each other it is difficult for them to interact. One of the reasons why the 'longwall' method of coal-mining was so disruptive of social relationships was that men had to work at considerable distances from each other. Physical closeness is not, of itself, enough to make individuals attractive to one another, of course. For some, the closer one's mother-in-law lives, the less attractive she becomes! Physical proximity then is a necessary, but not sufficient condition for attraction. Large physical distance is not the only factor in a work situation that can be disruptive of social interaction. Noise, for example, which prevents people talking to each other, is equally disruptive.

One important condition for group attraction reported by Lott and Lott (1965) is contact under conditions of cooperation. When the task requires the individuals to work together in order to achieve a successful outcome, there is evidence that this leads to the other members of the group being seen as attractive. Of critical importance, however, is the word 'successful'. For example, it is a common experience that football teams which are unsuccessful are often characterised by internal conflicts and scapegoating, especially where the lack of skill of certain individuals is seen as the cause of team failure. In addition, of course, the success has to be in a certain task which the individual feels worthwhile.

A further factor considered by Lott and Lott to be important in group attractiveness is the fact that being a member of a group involves a measure of group acceptance. To be accepted as a group member is to be valued as an individual and this is likely to lead to an increase in self-esteem. Furthermore, Van Zelst (1951) has shown that the more a worker is valued by his fellow workers the greater is his job satisfaction. Individuals who are liked by others also tend to be more satisfied with working conditions and other aspects of the job. However, the correlation of 0·82 found by Van Zelst between the degree to which an individual is popular and job satisfaction is extremely high and Van Zelst himself is cautious about the extent of the relationship. Nevertheless, the results do suggest that when an individual is attractive to others with whom he works, that individual is likely to be highly job satisfied. This again shows the importance of social factors in job satisfaction.

A further function of a group which may make it attractive to individuals is that it can give support in times of stress or threat. The isolated individual, for example, is relatively powerless against bullying by his superiors, but with group support the individual is far better able to withstand outside attacks of this kind. This, of course, is one of the main functions of a trade union.

Further reasons which have been advanced for the attractiveness of work-groups include the fact that they allow the attainment of goals not possible for the individual alone. The footballer cannot exercise his skills in isolation from others. Being a member of a group also allows the chance of comparing oneself with others, of gaining information about oneself and the world in general which would not ordinarily be obtained, and finding out how to behave in terms of the norms appropriate to particular situations. For example, it is well established that groups of workers will sometimes determine for themselves an appropriate work output in a particular situation, regardless of management desires. The classic example of this comes from the Hawthorne studies of the bank wiring room. The workers deliberately restricted their own output in order to prevent management reassessing the amount of output necessary for a particular piece-work payments system. Those who worked too hard had social sanctions brought against them as they were threatening the wellbeing of the other group members.

Groups are attractive in general terms, then, because they allow the individual to achieve a variety of goals, to receive social support, to increase self-esteem and to enjoy social interaction as a pleasure in its own right. Where the group provides these various needs for the individual, it is likely to be attractive to him. Where all members of the group perceive the group as offering rewards the group can be described as cohesive. Members of cohesive groups have been shown to be more job satisfied than those in groups which they do not perceive as being attractive. Adams and Slocum (1971), for example, found a relationship between degree of job satisfaction and degree of group cohesiveness. Interestingly, however, they found the relationship was only for employees with low levels of skill. This, of course, may reflect the fact that, for low level jobs, satisfaction with social aspects of the job is one of the major aspects of job satisfaction. For high level jobs, however, the actual job itself may be relatively more important in determining job satisfaction than is satisfaction with social interaction. Nevertheless, Adams and Slocum's conclusion should, perhaps, be treated with some caution as it is based on only thirty-three individuals. It is common experience that even in high level jobs there is satisfaction to be derived from 'on the job' social interaction and that interpersonal conflict, in particular, can reduce job satisfaction.

'Off the job' social relationships

Whilst the discussion up till now has concentrated on 'on the job' social relationships, a study by Gruneberg, Startup and Tapsfield (1974), suggests that 'off the job' social relationships can also influence satisfaction. In their study, of university teachers in Wales, they found that academics who had been to school locally were more job satisfied than those who had been brought up in other parts of the United Kingdom. Again, 62 per cent of those brought up locally believed that national geographical factors made a positive contribution to overall job satisfaction, whereas only 29 per cent of those brought up in other parts of the United Kingdom felt this. Many of those from outside Wales expressed feelings of isolation. 'One will always be an outsider in Wales to some extent,' was one comment. To move from one's area brings not only problems of practical adjustment – who is to babysit now, establishing friendships, and so on, which most people can cope with – it also brings problems of adapting to a different culture and of being 'on the outside'. Whilst the study of Gruneberg *et al.* is little more than suggestive, it does indicate the possibility that moving from one part of the country to another for reasons of employment may introduce social problems, reflected in job satisfaction.

Summary

The importance of social relationships at work for most individuals is almost self-evident. The study of Van Zelst (1952) shows that allowing individuals to choose their own work-mates improves satisfaction, whereas the study by Trist and Bamforth (1951) shows that disrupting social groups reduces job satisfaction. Individuals find work-groups attractive for a number of reasons: satisfaction gained through cooperating with others to achieve a goal, the satisfaction arising from feeling valued by others, the protection given by a group against outside threat, and the satisfaction gained from interaction with others as a pleasure in its own right – friendship. A number of studies, such as that of Adams and Slocum (1971), have shown a relationship between job satisfaction and the extent of group attractiveness. Their findings suggest that this is more important with the less skilled groups.

4 SATISFACTION WITH SUPERVISION

The importance of supervision

An aspect of work-group functioning which is of considerable importance concerns the relationship between the work-group and supervisor. As with pay, it is difficult to generalise about the importance of supervision on the job satisfaction of individuals. Certainly the 'Human Relations' school regarded supervision (that is, friendly supervision) as being of utmost importance in improving job satisfaction. Results of surveys, however, have been less clear cut. Herzberg *et al.* (1957), for example, in examining the findings of sixteen studies, found supervision to be ranked sixth in importance, behind such factors as security, wages, and intrinsic aspects of the job. However, as was noted in the discussion of the importance of pay, survey findings in this area are meaningless because of the influence of social desirability factors affecting ratings, of large discrepancies between studies and of general inadequacies in the design of many of the studies.

As with other variables that affect job satisfaction, it is likely that the importance of supervision will vary from situation to situation and from time to time. Vroom (1964), for example, cites evidence that there are often changes in satisfaction following changes in supervision. This is not difficult to imagine as new supervisors with new styles of leadership are likely to introduce changes which require individuals to change their habitual way of behaving. The 'new broom' is unlikely to be appreciated by those who have adapted to old methods. On the other hand, in situations where grievances abound, a new supervisor may be able to increase satisfaction by remedying sources of discontent. One reason why British universities usually appoint an external candidate as a new Head of Department may be because he is free from previous relationships with members of staff and is not, therefore, constrained to the same extent in making changes which disrupt previous ways of behaving. (In addition, he often has power on entering employment to demand new facilities as the price of accepting the post, a power which declines once he takes up the appointment.)

Employee and task-orientated supervision

As was noted previously, interest in the importance of supervision goes back to the 'Human Relations' school. In the Hawthorne experiment, increased productivity was associated with the increased friendliness of supervision. This was interpreted as indicating that increased friendliness of supervision led to increased job satisfaction which in turn led to increased productivity. Unfortunately, the causal relationship between friendly supervision and increased job satisfaction and productivity is unclear. It may well be that increased productivity led to friendlier supervision rather than the other way round. After all, the supervisor, no less than the operators, has goals to achieve. It is likely that when the supervisor's goal of increased productivity is achieved, he will then behave in a more relaxed and friendly manner.

A second major influence in the field of supervision was the classic experiment of Lewin, Lippett and White (1939). In their study, a group of boys was required to undertake tasks under three different styles of leader: authoritarian, democratic and laissez-faire. The authoritarian leader gave the boys tasks to do, he did not consult them in any decision and generally directed the work of the group without any attempt at social support. The democratic leader, on the other hand, took the wishes of individuals into account when allocating tasks, discussed various alternative problem-solving activities with the boys and gave encouragement and social support. The laissez-faire leader took little part in any decision-making process. The result of the experiment was a clear-cut preference on the part of the group members for democratic leadership.

In later studies of supervisory behaviour, a distinction has been made between employee- and task-orientated supervisors (e.g. Weed, Mitchell and Moffitt, 1976). These categories compare very roughly to democratic and authoritarian leaders, as does another categorisation frequently made between 'considerate' and 'initiating' leadership. An employee-orientated supervisor is one who establishes a supportive personal relationship with his workers, takes a personal interest in them and tries to ensure that they achieve their personal goals. The task-orientated supervisor, on the other hand, regards his group as instrumental in achieving production targets set by his employers and sees his main function as initiating and organising group work.

As Warr and Wall (1975) point out, employee-orientated and task-orientated supervision are not opposite sides of the same coin. It is possible for an individual to be interested in the welfare of his group *and* take an active part in organising the group to get the work done. He may, after all, be the most able member of the group and see the best interests of the group being served by organising and defining individuals' roles in certain aspects of the job. Warr and Wall argue that where someone is *very* high in task-orientation he will *in fact* be low in employee-orientation because in order to be considerate to employees one has to take account of their views and problems. One can, however, be *somewhat* orientated towards the task and still be high in employee-orientation.

Many studies have shown that most employees prefer considerate leadership. Thus, House, Filley and Kerr (1971) and Warr and Wall (1975) note a number of studies in which consideration in supervisors is related to job satisfaction. For example, a study by Sadler (1970) of computer personnel found that both males and females preferred a leader who consulted employees about decisions, although the preference was considerably greater for males than females. The relationship between supervisory style and job satisfaction has been reported in industrial plants, in military settings, in educational institutions, research laboratories and in Government Agencies. (It has also been shown, in a number of studies, that considerate leadership is related to productivity.) As Warr and Wall point out, however, it is hardly surprising that considerate leadership and job satisfaction are related, since an intrinsic aspect of considerate leadership is that the leader is 'pleasant' and 'nice'. Few people prefer others to be nasty to them. As with the Hawthorne study, many of the studies cited are correlational in nature, thus presenting the problem of direction of causality. It may be that supervisors display a greater consideration for subordinates whom they perceive as being satisfied and perhaps, therefore, more amenable and pleasant. Another problem, pointed out by Vroom, is that many studies rely on reports of subordinates in assessing leadership styles of supervisors. Thus, there is the problem that people tend to attribute to those they like pleasant characteristics which may not be objectively valid.

Another limitation on the general conclusion that employee-orientated leaders increase the job satisfaction of their subordinates, comes from the study by Foa (1957) who found that there are individuals with authoritarian personalities who prefer authoritarian, directed leadership. This is in line with the findings of Lewin, Lippett and White, that not all the boys in their groups preferred democratic leadership.

That not every individual wants the same from a supervisor has also been pointed out by House (1971). He noted that different groups of workers have different attitudes towards task-orientated leaders. Several studies have shown this kind of leadership to be resented by unskilled and semi-skilled workers, whereas among high level employees task-orientated leadership is positively related to satisfaction and performance. House suggests that this is because, for high level employees, a leader who is task-orientated can use his greater skill to help the group members attain their goals. For low level workers on the other hand, the skills required of the supervisor in enabling the individual to reach his goals are considerably less and the leader imposing a structure on the job is seen as an external control and limitation on behaviour. Of course, as noted before, being highly task-orientated in the case of high level employees does not rule out the possibility of being high on consideration also. Weed *et al.* (1976), for example, investigated three leadership styles, one high on human relations and low on task-orientation, one high on task-orientation and low on human relations and one high on both. They found the leader high on *both* task-orientation and human relations was liked the best.

The findings of House (1971) that for high level employees task-orientated leaders are appreciated, indicates that apart from human relations skills, other leadership skills are related to job satisfaction. After all, being nice and pleasant to one's subordinates is not *of itself* enough to ensure job satisfaction. There clearly are situations in which pleasantness of the supervisor is secondary to success in the task. Under enemy fire, for example, the soldier is not interested in how nice the officer is, but whether the leader can get him out alive with his skills. A study by Misshawk (1971) confirms, for example, that employees look for more than human relations skills in their supervisors, whatever their occupational levels. For high, medium and low level skill groups, Misshawk found that all regarded technical and administrative skills of importance to their job satisfaction in addition to human relations skills. An individual can be both authoritarian and technically competent, or participative and administratively incompetent, of course. Technical and administrative skills are independent of leadership style.

Summary

Whilst it is difficult to assess exactly how important leadership style is to job satisfaction, it does appear reasonable to suggest that different kinds of leadership style can have considerably different effects. A distinction is frequently made between employee- and task-orientated leaders and a large number of studies have shown a relationship between employee-orientated leadership and job satisfaction. As one aspect of employee-orientation involves dimensions such as 'pleasantness' the result is hardly surprising. What is more important, perhaps, is the finding that task-orientated leaders are not necessarily low on consideration for employees and that for high level groups there is a relationship between task-orientation and job satisfaction. This relationship has not been found for low level workers and indicates that great care must be taken when interpreting the relationship between leadership behaviour and job satisfaction. The extent to which the leader is instrumental in achieving the goals of the subordinate is critical in this context.

5 JOB SATISFACTION AND PARTICIPATION

Intimately related to the concept of supervisory style is the question of participation in decision-making. Thus, it was pointed out that in the Lewin, Lippett and White experiment, the democratic leader allowed group members to express their views, which were taken into account in decision-making. Considerate leadership, however, involves more than allowing individuals to participate in decision-making; it also involves dimensions of pleasantness and of taking an interest in the individual *as* an individual. It may therefore be the case that it is the 'pleasantness' aspect of considerate leadership that is related to job satisfaction rather than participation in decision-making.

Immediate participation

Warr and Wall make the useful distinction between participation which is immediate and which involves one's own immediate work-group, and distant participation which involves partici- pation in wider company policies.

As far as immediate participation is concerned, Lischeron and Wall (1975a) note that the correlational evidence certainly supports the view that the degree of perceived participation is related to employee satisfaction. For field studies, however, the evidence is far less compelling. Coch and French (1948), in their famous study on 'Overcoming resistance to change', found that involvement in participation resulted in increases in pro- ductivity. They did not, however, provide any statistically sig- nificant evidence on the effects on job satisfaction. A second study by French, Israel and As (1960), examined the effects of participation in decision-making on job attitudes and found that in only three out of fourteen items was there a significant improvement in job satisfaction.

The only major field study to have found effects of partici- pation on job satisfaction is that of Morse and Reimer (1956). Their study was based on increasing involvement in decision- making for one set of employees and reducing it for another. For the group given increased participation, there was a significant improvement in employee attitudes, for the reduced participation group the reverse was the case. However, for the participating group, there was no significant improvement in overall job satisfaction.

Given that the majority of immediate participation studies are correlational, and that field studies are far from convincing, Lischeron and Wall (1975a) warn against drawing the conclusion that a relationship between degree of participation and job satisfaction exists. Yet whilst correlational studies do not indicate the causal direction of a relationship, they do indicate that there is a relationship. Of course, it may be that the relationship is due to a factor associated with both variables. For example, it is possible that greater participation normally is associated with greater pleasantness of the leader, which is associated with greater job satisfaction. On the other hand, Lischeron and Wall's criticism that almost all studies focus on low level jobs seems reasonable, and makes generalisation to higher order jobs difficult.

It would not, of course, be surprising to find that participation in decisions immediately affecting the individual should increase job satisfaction. To have one's views considered and acted on is likely to increase one's self-esteem. It also allows more freedom to act in the way one thinks suitable for one's own abilities and thus increases potential for applying skill to a particular job. Certainly there is ample evidence that individuals do desire immediate participation. Hespe and Wall (1976), for example, found in their studies of nurses, local authority employees and industrial workers, that 60–70 per cent felt that they should be involved in immediate participation and that their views should be noted. At the very least, in the light of such evidence, it would be foolish to ignore the possibility that immediate participation is related to satisfaction.

Distant participation

Whilst the evidence on immediate participation and job satisfaction is at least suggestive, the same cannot be said of the relationship between job satisfaction and distant participation (participation in the general policy-making of an organisation). This is a fashionable political cause at present with all three major political parties in Great Britain pledged to increasing industrial democracy to a greater or lesser extent. Social scientists, union officials and industrialists have all added their voices to those of the politicians. Yet, as Hespe and Wall point out, there is one voice which is noticeable by its absence, namely that of the employee himself, and the research which exists sometimes shows only a limited interest on the part of employees in participation programmes. They note that distant participation schemes are often imposed on workers either by politicians, trade union leaders or management, so that lack of support for participation in higher level decisions may reflect disinterest in particular schemes which have been foisted on employees.

Hespe and Wall's own work, however, shows that there is a desire for participation in decision-making at a medium and distant level. Startup and Gruneberg (1973), in their study of the job satisfaction of university teachers, also found considerable desire for participation in university policy-making at all levels of teaching staff. For example, 52 per cent of senior lecturers and 45 per cent of lecturers wished to play a greater part in university policy-making. Surprisingly, 30 per cent of professors also wished to play a greater part, indicating, perhaps, that even those of a professorial status feel limited in the amount of organisational control which they exercise.

As far as experimental evidence on the relationship between distant participation and job satisfaction is concerned, Lischeron and Wall (1975a) report a lack of evidence. They investigated the effect of distant participation on blue collar employees working for a local authority (1975b). The participation involved each individual being given the chance to express his views by personal contact with superiors through a system of Action Planning Groups (APG). These groups consisted of between six and fourteen men, together with their immediate superior and a representative from management. The meetings lasted approximately one hour and took place every three weeks. Individuals were encouraged to raise grievances and ask for information. This the management undertook to supply, if not at the meeting in which the question was raised, then at a subsequent meeting. The effect of the APGs was undoubtedly to increase the influence of the men on decisions being made by management. For example, changes were made to the design of equipment, to the supply of materials and to procedures for ordering work from outside organisations. There was no change to the bonus system nor is there any report of any fundamental change in work design, or in supervisory practices.

After five months, the effect of participation on job satisfaction was measured. The investigators found no increase in job satisfaction overall, or with respect to pay, promotion, the job itself, the organisation, immediate superiors or co-workers, although there was a significant increase in satisfaction with management. There was also considerable satisfaction with the APG system and most employees wanted the scheme to continue.

How, then, does one account for the failure of the scheme to affect job satisfaction? One possible response is to take the line of Lischeron and Wall who argue that there is no direct or strong causal relationship between participation and job satisfaction. They regret the conclusion drawn by many other investigators of an established relationship. Certainly it does appear on the basis of Lischeron and Wall's study, that there is no *necessary* relationship.

On the other hand, it is clear that, in the study of Lischeron and Wall, few changes of real significance appear to have been achieved by the APGs. Perhaps one should look at the value of participation in the way that House (1971) looks at supervision, that is, in terms of how instrumental it is in achieving the individual's goals. Where participation results in major and direct changes, then perhaps it will be seen to affect job satisfaction. On the other hand, the results of Lischeron and Wall's study indicate that providing a talking shop, *per se*, is no prescription for increasing job satisfaction. Indeed, it might well be that where the opportunity for participation reveals limitations in influence, the experience of participation could lead to dissatisfaction. Certainly, Lischeron and Wall seem to have demonstrated that any assumption about participation leading to greater job involvement, and in turn leading to greater job satisfaction, is invalid.

It is not necessarily the case, however, that the value of participation should be seen only in terms of the individual becoming more job involved and hence more job satisfied. In the study of Startup and Gruneberg (1973), in response to the question 'Would you like persons of a similar status to yourself to have a greater part in the university policy-making?' the percentage of positive responses for senior lecturers and lecturers was 80·6 per cent and 63·8 per cent, respectively. This represents a significantly greater proportion than those who wanted to participate in university policy-making themselves. This kind of finding is important since it indicates that what is important about the participation process for many individuals is not the taking part in decision-making as such, but rather the feeling that their interests are being properly represented. Indeed within a university situation, participation in decision-making committees is often seen as being a boring exercise which intrudes on the time available for research and other desired activities and which should be avoided where possible.

Summary

Participation in decision-making is of two kinds: participation in immediate aspects of the job and participation in distant aspects. From surveys, there is considerable correlational evidence for the relationship between immediate participation and job satisfaction but field studies are far from convincing. As far as distant participation is concerned, there appears to be little evidence to support any causal relationship between participation and job satisfaction as such. On the other hand, participation schemes do appear popular with employees. However, they may be important not so much because of participation *per se*, but because individuals feel their interests are best represented in this way in their dealings with management.

It must be noted, however, that what is wanted by employees is not necessarily wanted by managers. To give others a say in decision-making is to reduce one's own powers. In addition, of course, the extra time taken in committee may interfere with efficient functioning. On balance, however, it does seem reasonable to suppose that opening up avenues of communication is likely to increase the data base upon which good decision-making can be grounded, and is a major means of providing feedback both to employees and management, a feature of 'good' jobs according to Hackman and Lawler (1971).

6 JOB SATISFACTION AND ROLE CONFLICT

Related to the question of how a supervisor carries out his role is the question of role conflict and role ambiguity. An inadequate supervisor who fails to agree with members of the group on exactly what goals are expected of them or how they should be carried out, will create feelings of uncertainty and insecurity. In addition, the possibility of role conflict arises where the performance of one individual is in conflict with that of another. Various studies of the relationship between role ambiguity and job satisfaction have been carried out and the results generally indicate that both role ambiguity and conflict lead to job dissatisfaction (e.g. Keller, 1975). Keller also showed role ambiguity to be associated with low levels of satisfaction with the work itself, whereas role conflict was associated with lower levels of satisfaction with supervisory behaviour, pay and promotion. He suggests that where a supervisor is inadequate in improving employees' working conditions, this will increase the likelihood of conflict.

A number of studies have examined factors which affect role conflict, role ambiguity and job satisfaction. One study for example, Johnson and Stinson (1975), found that those with a high need for achievement were more affected by role ambiguity and conflict. Presumably those who have no high involvement in the job and do not see the job as fulfilling any of their important needs are less frustrated about any difficulties in adequate job performance. Schuler (1977) found those with higher ability were less affected by role ambiguity. Presumably the greater the ability of the individual, the better he will be able to work out ways of coping with an ambiguous situation. The evidence on role conflict, ambiguity and job satisfaction is therefore reasonably clear in showing that job satisfaction can be affected by these variables and that personality factors are also important in considering the effects of role conflict and ambiguity on job satisfaction.

As Keller points out, the findings in this area have clear practical implications. Where a supervisor fails to agree with a subordinate as to which role should be performed, the uncertainty can lead to a lowering of job satisfaction. Similarly, employers should make clear exactly what criteria are required in order to obtain promotion and salary increases. An important aspect of making role expectations clear, therefore, is to ensure that individuals are inducted into an organisation in such a way that their roles and those of others in the organisation are made clear. It has already been noted (Chapter 1) how induction procedures can influence job satisfaction. Making roles explicit is probably one reason for this.

7 ORGANISATIONAL STRUCTURE AND CLIMATE

The study of supervisory behaviour has led to a distinction between democratic and authoritarian supervision. Democratic supervisors take the views of subordinates into account, take account of the values, feelings and needs of subordinates, and seek to improve their wellbeing at work. Authoritarian supervisors, on the other hand, make decisions without consultation and seek to maximise the goals of the organisation without taking account of the welfare of subordinates. Not only small groups, however, but whole organisations can be described in terms of whether or not they are authoritarian and task-orientated at the expense of individual needs. Such authoritarian organisations are known as bureaucratic structures, and, according to Argyris (1973), comprise the majority of organisations.

Bureaucratic structures are organisational structures which are hierarchical in nature, such that there is a progression from the least powerful to the most powerful as one ascends the organisational hierarchy. In addition, bureaucratic structures are usually pyramid-shaped, with large numbers of individuals on the lowest rungs of the organisation ladder, and only a few people at the top exercising control. One of the characteristics of a bureaucratic structure is that production jobs should be as deskilled as possible, so that they can be performed by practically anyone with a minimum of training. This will lead to efficiency as people can be moved from one job to another very easily. Such efficiency is obviously better where human relationships are impersonal, otherwise people might be reluctant to move from one job to another, and Gordon (1970) argues that impersonalisation is one of the characteristics of bureaucracies. Another characteristic of bureaucracies is that decision making concerning job content is taken at higher levels, so that workers are required to perform jobs without, in many cases, the opportunity to participate in decision making about them. This leads to another aspect of bureaucracies, that individuals will tend to do what they are told, and stick rigidly to their given roles. (See Payne and Pugh (1976) for a detailed discussion of organisation structure.)

A typical example of a bureaucratic structure might be in the car industry, where, at the lowest levels, a large number of people are involved in relatively unskilled assembling of parts on a moving conveyor belt. In charge of a group of such men is a supervisor, and in charge of the supervisors are lower levels of management, who in turn are responsible to higher levels of management and so on. As Walker and Guest (1952) noted, (see Chapter 3), many jobs on the conveyor belt offer little in the way of task variety, or task autonomy of meaningfulness, and many of the workers they studied were frustrated by the nature of their jobs. Hackman and Lawler (1971) too, noted the importance of such factors in job satisfaction, and Argyris (1973) has argued that it is this aspect of bureaucratic structure which conflicts with the needs of individuals for fulfillment. The kinds of job change discussed in Chapter 7, involving job enlargement and enrichment, have been advocated by writers such as Argyris to overcome the problems of lack of variety, autonomy and meaningfulness in low-level jobs.

As well as problems with the job itself, bureaucratic structures suffer from a number of other limitations which are likely to affect job satisfaction. In particular, because of their hierarchical structure, people at the bottom often have difficulty in communicating with those higher up who are making decisions concerning their jobs. Decisions are therefore more likely to be made which do not take into account the needs and welfare of those having to undertake the jobs. A further problem caused by a hierarchical organisation is that distance between top and bottom often means delays in communication, so that problems which arise can take a considerable time to put right, with a consequent effect on job satisfaction.

A further major problem with bureaucracies arises out of the assumption that relationships are of little importance, so that individuals can be moved from job to job as required. Such an assumption ignores the informal social relationships which everyone builds up at his place of work, and which for many people are a major source of satisfaction at work. To move people around as if such relationships were of no consequence is bound to lead to feelings of frustration and dissatisfaction. However, the importance of informal relationships goes much further than merely disrupting relationships. Communication within organisations depends on *people* communicating with one another, not on teleprinters communicating with each other. People have likes and dislikes, they have fears that some kinds of communication will lead to their being thought incompetent, and so on. Communications are therefore interpreted and selective. By failing to take account of human fallabilities, the hierarchical nature of bureaucracies is susceptible to communication blockages and subsequent frustrations when inadequate decision making follows.

It would, however, be wrong to assume that all aspects of bureaucratic structures are bad. Bureaucracies emphasise systems of rule to be followed, and in some situations it is essential that this takes place. Few individuals would wish to have a civil service whose every decision depended on small group discussions, and even for individuals within organisations, a system of rules and decision processes is often essential if there is to be order in the organisation. It is almost always the case that organisations are neither entirely bureaucratic nor entirely democratic in nature, but are more or less bureaucratic or democratic, depending on a number of factors, such as the nature of the product. For example, where the product and the production processes are stable, bureaucratic structures are more justifiable in terms of production efficiency (if not in terms of human welfare) than is the case where an organisation depends for its existence on the innovations and creativity of its workforce. Even so, the work of Hackman and Lawler (1971) and of many others casts doubt on whether bureaucratic organisation is best for any organisation, if it involves extensive deskilling of jobs.

Whilst much of the research effort on job satisfaction and organisation structure has recently centred on low-level jobs, Porter and Lawler (1964) have examined the effects of organisational structure on managerial job satisfaction. They found the question to be complex, with flat, non-hierarchical, non-bureaucratic structures providing greater satisfaction in relatively small organisations (under 5000 employees), but there was no relationship for large organisations. The different kinds of organisational structure provided for the satisfaction of different needs, with tall bureaucratic structures providing greater satisfaction of security needs and flat structures providing greater satisfaction of higher-order needs.

It is, of course, not surprising that different organisational structures should provide for the satisfaction of different needs. Bureaucratic structures, where rules are clearly laid down, and where everyone has his place, are likely to appeal more to individuals who have strong needs for security, and Gordon (1970) argues that the matching of bureaucratically orientated individuals to bureaucratic structures is likely to result in increased job satisfaction. On the other hand, creative individuals, and those who wish to take part in decision-making processes, are more likely to enjoy more democratic structures. Yet all organisations require some framework of rules to cope with co-ordination of activities. The reason why Porter and Lawler failed to find a relationship between job satisfaction and organisational structure for large organisations may, therefore, be that the dissatisfaction caused by lack of co-ordination outweighed the satisfaction obtained from freer controls in decision making.

One aspect of organisational structure which has an effect on job satisfaction, is, as noted above, organisational size. Porter and Lawler (1965) in fact found little empirical evidence on the topic, although Porter himself found that lower-level managers were more satisfied in smaller organisations whereas, for upper-level managers, the reverse was the case. Perhaps this is because higher-level managers would prefer to be big fish in big ponds rather than in small ponds, where pay, prestige and challenge are likely to be less. Perhaps a more important effect of size is, as noted earlier, that in large organisations problems of co-ordination become greater, hence making a bureaucratic structure more likely, with its consequent effects on job satisfaction.

Since the study by Porter and Lawler, a number of further studies have examined the influence of organisational structure on job satisfaction. Carpenter (1971), for example, found that teachers preferred flat organisational structures and were more job-satisfied than those in tall structures. Ivanecevich and Donelly (1975) found salesmen in flat organisations to have a higher job satisfaction, to report lower amounts of anxiety and to perform more efficiently than those in tall organisations. It seems clear from the evidence that for smaller organisations at least, job satisfaction is greater where the organisational structure is flat, bearing in mind the fact that there are individual differences in what satisfies people in their jobs.

Organisational Climate and Job Satisfaction

Closely related to the nature of organisational structure is the nature of organisational climate. This has been described by Schneider and Snyder (1975) as the global impression that people have of what an organisation comprises. It does, however, involve a number of dimensions, such as the degrees of risk taking, warmth, support, control, morale and progressiveness of the organisation, all of which, of course, depend on the underlying organisational structure. Bureaucratic structures, as was noted above, will tend to be low on all but the control dimension of these aspects of organisational climate.

A number of investigators have examined the relationship between organisational climate and job satisfaction. Friedlander and Margulies (1969), for example, found that satisfaction with task involvement was greatest in climates, high in management thrust (getting the organisation moving) whereas satisfaction with interpersonal relationships was highest in organisations where the climate was low in routine, burdensome duties. An important finding was that there are individual differences in satisfaction with organisational climates. Amongst those for whom work is highly valued, satisfaction is high in organisations with management thrust. For those who place a greater emphasis on social factors in work, satisfaction is greater in those organis-ations which place an emphasis on a pleasant social climate. Friedlander and Margulies also found organisational climate affected satisfaction with personal relationships more than other aspects of satisfaction. They conclude, therefore, that organis-ational climate should be viewed as a social and interpersonal phenomenon, and suggest that satisfaction can be heightened for social and interpersonal factors by improving the social environ-ment and management thrust, and by reducing the number of routine and burdensome tasks.

Pritchard and Karasick (1973) in their study of the re-lationship between organisational climate and job satisfaction, also found significant correlations between job satisfaction and aspects of organisational climate such as supportiveness, concern for social relationships and so on. As with the study of Friedlander and Margulies they also found individual differences in the relationship between job satisfaction and organisational climate. High-autonomy managers, not surprisingly, were considerably more satisfied in climates low in decision centralisation.

More recently Schneider and Snyder (1975) again examined the relationship between organisational climate and job satisfaction. They found differences in correlations between measures of job satisfaction and organisational climate for a number of different groups, such as managers, secretaries and supervisors in an insurance office. For example, the correlation between satisfaction with work and a climate of harmony was significant for managers but not for secretaries. The correlation between a climate of 'support' and satisfaction with supervisors was not significant for managers, but very much so for trainees. Such findings, and the findings of Friedlander and Margulies, and Pritchard and Karasick, on individual differences on the effects of organisational climate on job satisfaction make it difficult to draw any firm conclusions at present on the relationship between job satisfaction and organisational climate. This is perhaps not surprising, given the complex nature of the concept.

SUMMARY AND CONCLUSIONS

This chapter has considered the major context factors which have been shown to affect the individual's feelings about his job. Whilst a large number of studies have asked individuals to rate different aspects of their jobs in terms of importance, this exercise is, at best, only valid for the particular group under investigation. One cannot generalise from the findings of one group to the findings of another. Reviewers who try to take an average rank of importance from different occupational groups are wasting their time. Cross study comparisons are impossible where different research workers have asked different questions in different ways to different populations differing in the work they do. What one can conclude is that in particular circumstances, each of the factors considered in the chapter is important to individuals in relation to their job satisfaction. Exactly how important each factor is will depend, amongst other things, on the personality of the individual and the way the organisation deals with the factor and the social context in which the factor arises.

The evidence has clearly shown that factors such as pay and supervision are complex factors which require careful analysis if their relationship to satisfaction is to be appreciated. The amount of pay one receives is not merely valued for what goods one can buy, but it is also an indication of the value the organisation places on an individual. Nor is the adequacy of pay judged in absolute terms, but rather in terms of how much the individual has received in relation to the rewards of others similar to himself. Even this is not the whole story, however, as individual levels of aspiration are also likely to affect satisfaction with pay.

Another factor clearly important to the individual is the social interaction he obtains with his fellow workers. Yet here too, interpretation of the evidence is complex. It appears, for example, that social interaction is much more important for lower than for higher level jobs.

One aspect of social relationships at work concerns the relationship between supervisory behaviour and job satisfaction and shows the limitations which have to be placed on any general statement about the best kind of supervisor. Not only do individuals differ in their preferences but different individuals at different occupational levels react differently to different kinds of supervisory behaviour.

Related to the question of supervisory style is the question of the degree to which those lower down the scale should be allowed to participate in decision-making affecting the organisation. The results of Lischeron and Wall's study (1975b) suggest that, contrary to the common assumption, participation has no necessary relationship with job satisfaction. The reason for this might well be that participation in decision-making is only satisfying if it can be seen to lead to changes within the organisation of major significance to the individual.

Another aspect of supervisory behaviour is the extent to which the group members are given adequate guidance on the work role expected of them. The study of Keller (1975) amongst others, shows the effect of poor role definition on job satisfaction.

Not only at a small work group level, but at an organisational level, the way in which the organisation is structured can affect job satisfaction, but in rather complex ways, as Porter and Lawler (1964) have shown. Only for smaller organisations, for example, is there a relationship between organisational structure and job satisfaction. Organisational structure also affects organisational climate, but the relationship between organisational climate and job satisfaction is at present unclear.

This chapter, then, indicated that a variety of factors other than the job itself can influence job satisfaction in important ways. Both job and context factors must be taken into account in an understanding of job satisfaction.

5 Job Satisfaction and Individual Differences

One of the arguments often brought against theories of job satisfaction is that they take little account of differences between people. Not everyone, for example, wants a job in which he can find fulfilment, some prefer jobs which give the highest financial return. What is wanted by one group of individuals in terms of a job is often different from what is wanted by another group.

In this chapter, the question of how differences between individuals affect their job satisfaction will be developed further. It must be noted at the outset, however, that a great many of the findings are inconsistent and that the research on this aspect of job satisfaction is perhaps less satisfactory than in other areas. Nevertheless, it is instructive to examine the findings, if only to appreciate how limited our knowledge is. The factors to be considered are differences in age, sex, tenure, cultural background and personality.

JOB SATISFACTION AND AGE

The general finding reported by Herzberg *et al.* (1957) on the relationship between job satisfaction and age, shows that job satisfaction starts high, declines, and then starts to improve again with increasing age. This relationship has basically been found in male populations but a recent study by Glenn, Taylor and Weaver (1977) indicates that female job satisfaction also increases with increased age. It should be pointed out, however, that other researchers, such as Hunt and Saul (1975), failed to find any relationship between job satisfaction and age for female workers, although they did find the hypothesised U-shaped curve for male workers. The results in this area are clearly inconsistent.

There are a number of exceptions to the findings of a U-shaped curve describing the relationship between age and job satisfaction, e.g. Hulin and Smith (1965). Saleh and Otis (1964) found that job satisfaction declined for some five years before retirement. They explained this decline as being due to a blockage in the possibilities of growth and achievement. For example, older individuals are often passed over for promotion and have to take orders from younger people. Another possibility put forward by Saleh and Otis is a decline in physical health which may result in less adequate job performance. Whatever the reason for the decline in job satisfaction, the distancing of an individual from his job may be a good way of adjusting to impending retirement. The less satisfied the individual is with the job he is leaving, perhaps the greater the potential for enjoying retirement.

A number of possibilities have been advanced to explain the results of increasing job satisfaction with age, up to the pre-retirement age, at least. Herzberg *et al.* (1957), for example, suggest that job satisfaction increases with age because the individual comes to adjust to his work and life situation. Job satisfaction is initially high but declines as expectations are not met, only to rise again as the individual again adjusts to his work situation. The generality of the results must be questioned, however. As was noted when considering the work of Van Maanen and Katz (Chapter 2), in different occupations there are differences in patterns of satisfaction over time so that generalisations from one study to another are dangerous. As was further noted with the Van Maanen and Katz study, there are considerable problems in interpreting the data. It may not be age, *per se*, but the increased opportunity older workers have had to find the job which suits them most, which is related to job satisfaction.

A second major problem in interpreting the experimental findings is that individuals at different ages are members of different reference groups. For example, methods and levels of education, moral values, cultural background, and life experiences are all different at different age levels in the population. Therefore, values and expectations at different age levels will be different. It was seen in Chapter 2 that the way other people felt about their job affected what the individual expected and was satisfied with. Clearly, age differences may be due to different values that different groups of individuals have because of their life experiences. If this is the case, it would not necessarily follow that individuals who are young today will become more job satisfied as they get older.

Bearing in mind the difficulties in interpreting results of studies on ageing and job satisfaction, it does appear that those entering employment tend to have higher levels of job satisfaction initially. This is important since it indicates that there is a potential of good will towards a job which the employer can build on. Such high levels on entering employment may be a consequence of heightened self-esteem caused by entering the 'adult' world, being independent and getting away from the regimentation of school and its association with boring lessons. Little wonder, then, that dissatisfaction sets in at work which soon becomes as boring as school, where financial independence gives way to financial problems on taking on family responsibilities and where the realities of limitations in career growth become apparent. The greater job dissatisfaction of this group would appear sometimes to manifest itself in counterproductive behaviour (see Chapter 6) so that it is important for management to realise the potential problems of younger workers. At the same time, it is essential to realise that the pattern of satisfaction as a function of age is likely to differ from occupation to occupation and possibly between the sexes. Again, as Hunt and Saul (1975) note, it is difficult to see why the kind of explanation given above for the increase in job satisfaction with age, does not apply consistently to females.

JOB SATISFACTION AND TENURE

Related to the question of age and job satisfaction is the question of tenure and job satisfaction. Wild and Dawson (1972), for example, found job satisfaction to be related to both age and length of service. With increased length of service the importance to job satisfaction of factors such as self-actualisation and conditions of work decreases, but the importance of pay increases. The relationship between job satisfaction and tenure is by no means clear, however. For example, job satisfaction has been shown by Hulin and Smith (1970) to increase with increased tenure. Gibson and Klein (1970), however, showed a decrease in satisfaction with increased tenure and attributed this to a realisation that the rewards on the job are not going to be as great as they expected.

Gibson and Klein's study was of blue collar workers and they suggest that frustration at seeing others promoted to management positions may increase dissatisfaction. On the other hand, when length of service was held constant, they found that job satisfaction was greater with increased age, confirming the general findings noted above. It should be noted, however, that controlling for length of service in an organisation still leaves open the possibility that older workers have had more experience, enabling them to select the kind of job which will satisfy them, based on their previous work history.

Whilst the evidence on the relationship between age and tenure and job satisfaction tends to indicate a relationship such that the older the individual and the longer he is in an organisation, the more job satisfied he is, the conclusions of Hunt and Saul (1975) are worth recording:

The research has highlighted the impracticality of attempting to develop a simple statement of the relationship between criteria of job satisfaction and employee age and tenure in an organisation . . . it is clear that the relationships studied are considerably influenced by the type of sample and the particular satisfaction criteria involved. Personality variables such as the level of job performance and the effects of age and tenure in an organisation's reward system appear to play major parts in determining the nature of the empirical relationship observed between measures of age, tenure and job satisfaction (p. 701).

JOB SATISFACTION AND SEX DIFFERENCES

As with age, the findings on the relationship between job satisfaction and sex are inconsistent. Some studies have found females to be more satisfied than males, some have found males to be more satisfied than females: some have found no difference (see Hulin and Smith, 1964). Clearly the research results do not permit any very firm conclusions to be drawn.

There is some evidence that males and females differ in what they expect from a job. Schuler (1975), for example, found that the females in his study valued the opportunities to work with pleasant employees more than males, whereas males regarded the opportunities to influence important decisions and direct the work of others as more important. Other researchers have confirmed Schuler in showing females to rate some aspects of the job as more important than males. Herzberg *et al.* (1957), also noted sex differences in the importance assigned to different aspects of the job, in so far as males regarded intrinsic job aspects as more important than females did. Later research of Manhardt (1972) and Bartol (1974) has shown males to be more concerned with their long-term careers. Again, however, the results are not entirely consistent as a study by Brief and Oliver (1976) failed to show any sex differences in work attitudes when controlling for occupation and organisational level.

Results of research in this area, then, often show sex differences in orientation to jobs, with females being less concerned with career aspects and more concerned with social aspects of the job. Schuler interprets the research findings as showing that the traditional role of females as empathetic and person-orientated shows in their job orientation, whereas males orientate more towards competitiveness.

Not only is it probable that males and females differ in their job orientation, they also differ in the way they are treated in the organisation. For example, Hulin and Smith (1964) point out that females are likely to be paid differently, have different opportunities for promotion and have different levels of job. Were these changed, Hulin and Smith argue, then females might well be as satisfied as males. In their study, females were generally less satisfied with their jobs than males.

However, as has been noted previously, job satisfaction depends on the extent to which the job is able to provide the employee with what he wants. Changing promotional opportunities and job level are unlikely to affect female job satisfaction if it does not result in changes in what females want from their jobs. For women who work for social reasons, for example, making a job more demanding might mean less opportunity for the kind of social contact they find rewarding.

Inconsistencies in findings on sex and job satisfaction can therefore be due to a variety of factors. Not only might males and females in the same organisation differ in job level, promotion prospects, pay and so on, in different occupations, they may differ in the extent to which the same job satisfies their needs. A job high on social satisfaction but low on skill utilisation and career prospects may result in higher job satisfaction for females than for males, whereas in occupations allowing little scope for social relationships, the differences in satisfaction might be in the opposite direction.

It is, however, important to take care when making generalisations on the basis of present research findings. Some researchers have argued that females are less appropriate occupants of managerial positions because of their different work attitude. In view of the inconsistency of the present research, of changes in social values associated with women working, and of large individual differences in work values, such an attitude is unwarranted. The research findings at best reaffirm what has been noted earlier: that not everyone wants the same out of a work situation and that different groups have different work attitudes.

JOB SATISFACTION AND EDUCATIONAL LEVEL

As was noted in Chapter 3, ability has been shown to be related to job satisfaction. For example, individuals of high ability may be more dissatisfied with jobs which do not allow for the application of their talents. As far as educational level is concerned, a study by Vollmer and Kinney (1955) showed this effect. They investigated the effect of level of education on the job satisfaction of individuals, and they examined the responses of several thousand civilian ordinance employees in various institutions throughout America. Their results indicated that more college than high-school-educated employees reported dissatisfaction with their jobs. Similarly more high-school-trained workers reported dissatisfaction than lower trained grammar-school-educated workers. Vollmer and Kinney argue that, because of the greater educational investment it is reasonable to assume that college-trained workers generally expect 'more out of life' in terms of higher paid jobs, better working conditions, etc. Thus for relatively low level jobs, they have higher expectations of what a job should offer and, therefore, lower satisfaction with what they get.

Similar findings to those of Vollmer and Kinney were reported by Klein and Maher (1966), who studied the pay satisfaction of college-educated and non-college-educated managers. Again they found non-college-educated managers to be more satisfied with pay than college-educated managers. Klein and Maher point to the importance of reference groups and argue that college-educated managers will relate their pay to their college contemporaries. Many feel that they are not doing as well. Non-college-educated managers, on the other hand, might feel that in relation to other non-college-educated individuals, their pay compares favourably. Furthermore, college-educated managers may refer more to external reference groups outside the company than do non-college-educated managers.

The results of the studies of Vollmer and Kinney and of Klein and Maher are to some extent at variance with the studies reviewed by Herzberg *et al.* (1957), who found some studies to show a positive relationship between educational level and job satisfaction. Klein and Maher argue, however, that such studies are somewhat restricted in their sampling, to very specialised groups of individuals. Yet it would not necessarily be surprising to find a positive relationship between education and job satisfaction. A large number of studies have shown that there is increased job satisfaction with increasing occupational level and clearly, the higher the education, the likelier it is that one will be at a higher occupational level.

The evidence, therefore, points to the complex nature of the relationship between educational level and job satisfaction. With respect to the implications of the various findings, Vollmer and Kinney emphasise the fact that selecting the best qualified candidate for a job is not necessarily the best decision to make. To have someone over-qualified in terms of the utilisation of skills is likely to lead to dissatisfaction when expectations or values on the job are not fulfilled. It is, therefore, vitally important that employers do not deceive themselves as to the demands required from a particular job. The tendency to increase the status of a job by increasing the academic qualifications necessary for entry, is clearly one which is fraught with problems.

The findings on the relationship between the level of education and job satisfaction also raise the question of whether it is advisable for the country to educate large numbers of its youth in university institutions. Whilst graduates may be better able to obtain jobs than non-graduates, the days are gone in most countries where a university graduate can count on getting the job he wants. Graduates now have to accept jobs below their expectations in terms of working conditions, pay, and the actual job they are employed to do. For example, in Britain, the number of graduates in psychology has grown so much over the last ten years or so that few can expect to enter occupations such as clinical or educational psychology. The great majority will have to accept jobs outside psychology where their skills may not be utilised. It is difficult, however, to see how people can be prevented from following educational careers of their choice, especially as the major function of education is the development of a person as an individual. Individuals should be made aware, however, that their education may not lead to the vocation of their choice.

JOB SATISFACTION AND CULTURAL DIFFERENCES

Racial differences

One major cultural factor which has received attention recently is the difference in job attitudes of blacks and whites. Jones *et al.* (1977), for example, matched black and white sailors in terms of the kind of job which they were doing. They found no differences in reported general satisfaction with their jobs, although black sailors did report higher satisfaction with pay and the opportunities to get a better job in the Navy. The findings of other research workers in the area are inconsistent. Some have found that whites report higher levels of job satisfaction, others the reverse.

As Jones *et al.* point out, one reason for the inconsistencies in results is that many studies compared individuals in different working conditions. It might therefore have been differences in working conditions alone which accounted for differences in job satisfaction. For example, if black workers are being paid less, given less interesting jobs, and fewer chances of promotion, then it would not be surprising to find greater satisfaction among white workers. On the other hand, Jones *et al.* found support for the view that blacks and whites bring different expectations to jobs, with blacks having lower expectations which are more easily met. In an area of high unemployment, therefore, a job which offers promotion opportunities and the use of skills may appear relatively more attractive to black than white workers, given their different expectations concerning the job. It is not surprising, then, that some studies found blacks, and some found whites, to enjoy greater job satisfaction. While Jones *et al.*'s study is important in suggesting that, with similar jobs, intrinsic satisfaction experienced by blacks and whites may be similar, it is clear that more than one study is required before any generalisations can be made.

The great majority of reported studies on blacks and whites are from American populations and these results reflect the difference in social climate, culture and opportunities as they exist in that country. Yet compared to South Africa, the United States is a relatively privileged country for blacks and the findings of the United States studies are not necessarily applicable in South Africa. Recently Orpen and Ndlovu (1977) examined the job satisfaction of clerks in commercial organisations in South Africa who engaged in routine work. As with the Jones *et al.* study, the authors showed blacks to be more job involved than whites. More importantly, they found blacks had significantly greater higher order needs and the correlation between participation and satisfaction was significantly greater amongst blacks than whites. Thus the greater the blacks participated in decision-making the greater was their satisfaction with their jobs. As Orpen and Ndlovu point out, such findings make nonsense of South African racial policies which seek to keep blacks down on the grounds that they have no interest in higher order jobs.

As with other areas of research into job satisfaction, the question of black-white differences is clearly complex. Studies which do not match individuals in terms of the job they are doing are clearly worthless. On the other hand, blacks and whites have a different reference group in terms of work values and expectations so that the way that these interact with particular jobs will produce different results. Clearly, however, there is evidence that black workers can be more satisfied, more job involved and can have greater higher order needs than their fellow whites working in similar occupations.

Rural and urban backgrounds

Hulin and Blood (1968) examined responses of workers from rural and urban backgrounds to various aspects of their job. They found that workers from a rural background were less alienated from their jobs than those from an urban background. As a consequence, workers from rural backgrounds reacted favourably to job enlargement programmes aimed at increasing the interest of the job, whereas workers from urban communities often responded negatively. They also found differences between blue and white collar workers and found that blue collar workers tended to be more alienated than white collar workers. One explanation of these findings is that white collar workers might relate back to a culture in which there is a strong ethic to work and to derive satisfaction from work. This is an ethic which may not exist for urbanised blue collar workers for whom there is such general alienation from middle-class values that they do not seek rewards from the job, and regard jobs as basically instrumental in providing money for 'off the job' activities. Attempts at job enlargement, therefore, are not seen as relevant to satisfying such individuals' needs.

Whilst the question of job enlargement will be discussed more fully in Chapter 7, the findings of Hulin and Blood have serious implications for job satisfaction. If workers from urban areas are not interested in their jobs, but only in financial and other low level rewards, then this might well influence company policy in siting new manufacturing plant.

The conclusions of Hulin and Blood have, however, been challenged on a number of points by Sussman (1973) and others. One of the main studies cited by Hulin and Blood, in support of a difference between urban and rural workers, is that of Turner and Lawrence (1965). Sussman points out however, that all the urban sample in this study were Catholic and this clearly limits the interpretation of the findings. The second major study cited was by Blood and Hulin (1967). This too, had a major methodological defect as they compared jobs which were likely to differ in work flow patterns and opportunities for promotion and social interaction. Clearly, when comparing urban and rural groups, the work characteristics must be similar. Despite these criticisms, Sussman does not deny the existence of differences between urban and rural communities in their attitudes to work. Both, in their different ways, in Sussman's study, appear amenable to changes in certain aspects of their job, however. Thus rural workers respond to greater job discretion with increased pride in accomplishment, whereas urban workers respond with greater general job interest. The evidence on the exact nature of the effect of workers' background on job attitudes is thus clearly conflicting and complex.

National differences

In addition to cultural differences, within countries, comparisons of job attitudes between countries have often been made. For example, in one study which compared Mexican and American workers, Slocum (1971) found Mexican operators to be significantly more job satisfied than their American counterparts who were undertaking similar jobs. In accounting for the results, Slocum argues that by and large Mexican workers are not highly motivated to work, once basic family needs have been met. The fulfilment of those needs, therefore, resulted in higher job satisfaction for Mexican workers. American workers, on the other hand, have higher expectations that higher order needs will be met on the job, and are dissatisfied with the fulfilment of only lower order needs.

The finding that American workers are less satisfied than Mexican workers contrasts with those discussed by Barrett and Bass (1976) who conclude that American workers usually report greater job satisfaction than, for example, German workers. Barrett and Bass point out the great problems of comparing like with like in terms of organisational structure in many of the studies and regard Slocum's study as one of the few which has controlled for most of the important plant differences (although there are methodological problems associated with the study). Findings such as those of Slocum certainly reinforce the arguments of Hulin and Blood concerning the importance of taking account of cultural and sub-cultural differences in examining attitudes to job satisfaction.

JOB SATISFACTION AND PERSONALITY DIFFERENCES

As Porter and Steers (1973) note in their resumé of the relationship between job satisfaction and turnover, there is a slight tendency for those individuals who leave organisations to have different personality characteristics from those who stay (see Chapter 6). Although such characteristics may or may not be related to job satisfaction, clearly the kind of person one is will determine the extent to which different job characteristics will affect one's job satisfaction. For example, the individual who is very ambitious is likely to be far more dissatisfied by a job where promotion is difficult compared to an individual whose main satisfaction in the job comes from social contacts.

Many writers point out that the relationship between personality factors and job satisfaction is very under-researched. Early work on boredom reported by Wyatt *et al.* (1934) led them to conclude that a number of personality factors such as calmness and a 'phlegmatic nature' were particularly suitable for repetitive work.

A study by Smith (1955) on the relationship between susceptibility to monotony and worker characteristics showed that workers susceptible to boredom tended to be 'restless in daily habits' and 'leisure time activities'. She failed to find any relationship between extraversion and susceptibility to boredom. A more recent study by Cooper and Payne (1967), however, did establish a relationship between non-permitted absence and both extraversion and neuroticism. As is noted in Chapter 6, absence does not necessarily indicate job dissatisfaction, but in the absence of other evidence, the findings of Cooper and Payne are suggestive.

Considerably more work has been undertaken on the relationship between the need for achievement and job satisfaction. McClelland (1961) emphasised the importance of the need for achievement in the behaviour of individuals in organisations. Among the conclusions reached were that those with high needs for achievement require jobs which challenge their abilities, so that success in the task increases self-esteem. Steers (1975) has recently conducted a number of studies on the effect of the need for achievement on job preference and satisfaction. In his studies he found that students with a high need for achievement showed higher relationships between job performance and job satisfaction than those with low needs for achievement. Steers argues that, for those with high achievement needs, superior performance is of itself a reward. Those with low achievement needs, on the other hand, do not see good performance as leading to greater job satisfaction. Perhaps they get their job satisfaction from social or other needs. Steers also argues that those individuals with high achievement needs will become involved in their jobs if they see the possibility that their jobs will lead to success and rewards.

A personality variable which may explain why those with high achievement needs are satisfied when they successfully perform their jobs is self-esteem. Warr and Wall describe self-esteem as the evaluation which a person makes about himself, indicating the extent to which he thinks of himself as capable, significant, successful and worthy. Many writers regard a reasonable level of self-esteem as important to mental health and one major determinant of self-esteem is undoubtedly occupational standing. An individual's self-esteem is likely to be greater where a comparison with other workers leaves him in a favourable position, it is likely to suffer where one compares unfavourably with one's reference group. As Warr and Wall note, an important aspect of self-esteem is that it is a concept that is easily understood and which makes the interpretation of organisational behaviour less complex. Job satisfaction is likely to be lower where the individual's self-esteem is threatened by being unable to apply skills, by being put in a situation where he compares badly with his fellows and so on. In addition, self-esteem is a characteristic of individuals some of whom are perhaps higher, some lower, on self-esteem than objective evidence would warrant.

Korman (1977) regards self-esteem as a critical personality factor in understanding job satisfaction. He argues that those with low self-esteem will not be satisfied as a result of task achievement, whereas for those who have a high level of self-esteem there will be a relationship between job performance and job satisfaction and he produces experimental evidence from a number of studies to support his claim. It also follows, presumably, that the individuals with high self-esteem will be more job dissatisfied when performance does not lead to rewards, as they will have a greater expectation that rewards should flow to them.

Locke (1976) argues that those with high self-esteem are more likely to value challenging tasks, are likely to experience fewer conflicts on the job and are less likely to value verbal recognition as a source of reassurance. The extent to which these are important 'on the job' factors affecting job satisfaction remains unclear at present.

SUMMARY

Whilst research on personality is of considerable importance, it is clear from the work reviewed in this chapter that a great deal remains to be done. For the most part, studies have shown small and inconsistent effects of variables such as age, sex role and personality variables on job satisfaction. Even differences in achievement need are admitted by Steers to have a relatively small effect on job attitudes. This is not to say that individual differences are not important, but the evidence does suggest that other organisational factors are more important at the present time. To some extent this may be because individuals initially select jobs from which they are likely to have some satisfaction whatever their personalities.

6 The Consequences of Job Satisfaction and Dissatisfaction

So far the effects of variables on job satisfaction have been discussed. The aim of the present chapter will be to consider how job satisfaction affects a variety of factors, some of economic and some of personal importance. Thus the consequences of job satisfaction for productivity, absence, turnover, counterproductive behaviour, health and life satisfaction will be considered in turn.

JOB SATISFACTION AND PRODUCTIVITY

One of the main reasons for studying job satisfaction is undoubtedly the widely held view that whether a person is satisfied or not with his job has consequences for his productivity, for his likely stay within the organisation and for his willingness to attend work regularly.

With respect to productivity, the Hawthorne studies were interpreted by proponents of the 'Human Relations' school as showing that, under friendly supervision, the individual increased his productivity as a consequence of increased satisfaction. Yet as was seen in the discussion of the Hawthorne experiment (Chapter 1), an equally plausible alternative is that as productivity increased, so did friendly supervision; satisfaction resulted from increased productivity, rather than caused it.

A number of reviews of the relationship between job satisfaction and productivity have cast serious doubts on the assumption that any relationship exists between the two factors. Brayfield and Crockett (1955), in their review of over fifty studies, found little overall relationship between satisfaction and productivity, a conclusion confirmed in a later review by Vroom (1964).

Two different arguments have been put forward to account for the apparent failure to find a relationship. Firstly, Herzberg considers that satisfaction may lead to increased productivity but that the wrong measures of satisfaction are often used. Secondly, Lawler and Porter (1969) suggest that, rather than higher satisfaction leading to higher productivity, it is higher productivity which leads to rewards which may or may not lead to increased satisfaction.

In accounting for the failure of studies to show a relationship between satisfaction and performance, Herzberg argues that it is basically motivators which give rise to satisfaction, and which are the key to increased performance. The failure to find a relationship in many studies is due to measures of satisfaction generally including measures of hygiene factors. As was seen in Chapter 2, Herzberg's theory is at best speculative, and the evidence provided by Herzberg on the satisfaction–performance relationship, must, therefore, also remain speculative.

In putting forward their expectancy theory, Lawler and Porter (1969) argue that, rather than increased satisfaction leading to performance, it is performance which leads to rewards which lead to satisfaction. The reason why the relationship between job performance and job satisfaction is often so low is that many individuals receive rewards from their jobs which have little to do with performance, or at least productivity. For example, the person who enjoys the social aspect of his work may get his rewards from talking to other co-workers and this, although increasing job satisfaction, may well be detrimental to productivity. In the Hawthorne studies, two girls in the first experiment had to be dismissed because their talking became so disruptive of the work.

The basic model of expectancy theory is given in Diagram 2.

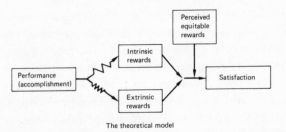

The theoretical model

DIAGRAM 2. The Effect of Performance on Job Satisfaction

From Lawler, E. E. and Porter, L. W. The effect of performance on job satisfaction, *Industrial Relations* (1969), 80, 20–8. Reprinted by permission.

As can be seen, the individual will receive job satisfaction from performance when that performance leads to rewards and when these rewards are perceived as equitable in terms of effort expended and comparison with the rewards of others. In other words, Lawler and Porter's theory incorporates the equity theory of job satisfaction in accounting for the relationship between performance and satisfaction. In addition, Lawler and Porter argue that the reward will lead to satisfaction to the extent that it is valued, and that intrinsic rewards will be more directly involved in the performance–satisfaction relationship. They support this suggestion by arguing that extrinsic rewards such as pay and benefits are not so directly related to effort and depend more on general company policy and group membership. The theory thus includes a number of theories of job satisfaction discussed in Chapter 2.

Expectancy theorists ask the question: 'What will make an individual work if it is not satisfaction, if satisfaction is a consequence, not a cause of productivity?' The answer is given in terms of the expectations individuals have that their efforts will lead to rewards. The individual will not be motivated to work in situations where he sees no relationship between performing a task and any actual reward. For example, a student will not be motivated to attend a lecture if the lecturer is so poor he cannot gain any useful information from attending.

In their model, Lawler and Porter also suggest that satisfaction will affect a worker's effort, arguing that increased satisfaction from performance possibly helps to increase expectations of performance leading to rewards. As Schwab and Cummings (1971) point out, however, so many factors affect whether satisfaction received will lead to increased performance in the future, that the performance–satisfaction relationship is likely to be stronger than the satisfaction–performance relationship.

A number of factors have been considered to be important in affecting the performance–satisfaction relationship. One of these is argued by Slocum (1971) to be the degree to which the individual has needs which require to be satisfied on the job. His study of steel-mill managers showed that the performance–satisfaction relationship was affected by the degree of need satisfaction. Furthermore, he found the higher order needs to be related to productivity more than the lower order needs, just as Lawler and Porter's theory would predict.

Hackman and Lawler (1971) found that satisfaction with four core dimensions of jobs (autonomy, variety, identity and knowledge of results) was positively related to productivity. Furthermore, the four dimensions were additive: the higher the composite score, the greater the job satisfaction and productivity. Again, as was claimed by Slocum, the strength of the higher order needs was found to affect the relationship between performance and satisfaction. Katzell and Yankelovich (1975), in a review of the relationship between job satisfaction and productivity, support Hackman and Lawler's view that the effect of job factors is additive. They argue for a critical mass approach to increasing job satisfaction and productivity, since changes in just one area of the job may produce little effect on either productivity or satisfaction. Only when a number of job dimensions are changed, is there likely to be a perceptible effect.

A number of further variables have been shown to affect the performance–satisfaction relationship. Among these are the degree of need for achievement (Steers, 1975) and self-esteem (Korman, 1977). Korman argues that the more an individual perceives himself as competent, the more he will see work performance as being a source of satisfaction. More important, perhaps, is another factor: the degree to which the individual has control over his work activity. It is self-evident that only where the individual has control is there a possibility of a relationship between job satisfaction and productivity.

In conclusion, therefore, it appears that whilst the 'Human Relations' approach to the job satisfaction–job performance relationship is inadequate, in that there is clearly no simple relationship, the gloomy view of there being no relationship between satisfaction and performance is also probably unwarranted. Where individual factors such as strength of need are taken into account, correlations between satisfaction and productivity are sometimes reported to be significant. The precise nature of the relationship between satisfaction and productivity remains unclear although it is obviously complex, and indeed, it may well be that performance causes satisfaction rather than the other way around.

JOB SATISFACTION AND WITHDRAWAL FROM THE WORKING ENVIRONMENT

One apparently self-evident result of job dissatisfaction is to increase the likelihood that the individual will withdraw from the work situation, either temporarily, by absenting himself for a short period of time, or permanently, by escaping from the organisation. Exactly how absence and employee turnover are related, however, is not entirely clear. Some research workers see absence as a miniature version of the decision taken to leave the organisation (see Herzberg *et al.*, 1957), and thus a sign that the individual is likely to leave in the near future. Other researchers (e.g. Hill and Trist, 1955), however, view absence as an alternative form of withdrawal behaviour to resignation, one that takes place, perhaps, when finding an alternative job is not a realistic possibility.

When examining the relationship between absence and turnover, Lyons (1972) found support for the view that absence was indeed a predicator of future termination of employment. Typical of the studies which he examined is one by Ronan (1963), in which 62 apprentices who left a programme over a ten-year period had higher absenteeism than the 137 who stayed. Unfortunately, the evidence is by no means unanimous. Argyle *et al.* (1957), for example, found no significant correlation between absence and turnover in ninety-eight work-groups, and a number of other studies have also failed to find any relationship. One reason for the contradictory nature of the results might be that only in a situation in which job alternatives are available are absence and turnover likely to be correlated.

It is not unreasonable to suppose that absence and turnover may have different causes. Porter and Steers (1973) point to various ways in which absenteeism and turnover are likely to be distinguishable. First, it is pointed out that the ill effects of absenteeism for the employee are likely to be less than that of leaving the job, assuming that no other job is available. For the employee, absenteeism may be cost-free since in many cases he may be paid for short absences, provided that some kind of excuse, such as illness, is given.

Secondly, to absent oneself from work is considerably less of a decision than is the decision to change jobs, with all the difficulties of re-adjustment and perhaps re-housing in another area. Finally, occupational mobility is necessary in certain careers, such as the academic, if promotion is to be attained. Leaving a particular job in such a situation would clearly have no implications concerning job satisfaction and is unlikely to be related to previous absence behaviour. Because of differences in their possible causes, absence and turnover are therefore considered separately.

JOB SATISFACTION AND ABSENCE

A number of reviews of the relationship between job satisfaction and absence have all concluded that there is a relationship although the magnitude of the relationship is small (e.g. Vroom, 1964; Porter and Steers, 1973). In the case of Porter and Steer's review of withdrawal behaviour, very few of the studies considered dealt with absence, and of those which did deal with absence, the study of Metzner and Mann (1952) found a relationship between satisfaction and absence for blue collar, but not for white collar workers. As Metzner and Mann note, their findings suggest there is no simple relationship between satisfaction and absence. In addition, Metzner and Mann note in passing that males and females differ significantly in their absence rate. Whilst this finding is not startling, it again suggests the importance of factors other than satisfaction in accounting for absence behaviour. Women, presumably, have more family commitments, such as having to look after young children when ill and are perhaps more susceptible to ailments (e.g. headaches), perhaps have less economic commitments and are perhaps less job involved.

Metzner and Mann's reservations concerning the lack of a simple and direct relationship between satisfaction and absence have received further support from two recent studies. Ilgen and Hollenbach (1977) found no relationship between absence and satisfaction in a group of female clerical workers in a university. They conclude that their results are not all that atypical and any positive correlations which exist are probably low. Furthermore, they point out that literature reviews are based almost completely on published work, whereas studies with negative findings are simply not published.

The most comprehensive review of the relationship between satisfaction and absence behaviour has been published by Nicholson *et al.* (1976). After reviewing twenty-nine studies, they conclude 'that the popular belief that job satisfaction is a major cause of absence from work has doubtful empirical validity'. In their analysis they claim that many of the studies showing a relationship are of doubtful scientific value for a number of reasons, and a number of those which are scientifically valid show no relationship, or at best a very low relationship. Their own study of over 1200 blue collar workers produced results in 'direct conflict with the view that job dissatisfaction is a major cause of industrial absence'. In other words, they found no evidence of any relationship.

Why, then, do the findings on the relationship between job satisfaction and absence fly in the face of the common-sense assumption that people happy in their jobs will attend work more regularly? A number of reasons have been suggested, apart from the obvious ones of geographical, weather and illness conditions not necessarily being related to job satisfaction. Ilgen and Hollenbach, for example, argue that it is unlikely that a high degree of satisfaction with pay, security and company policy will lead to regular attendance in organisations which have generous sick-leave schemes. In fact, they argue, company policies which allow for more frequent absences might produce greater satisfaction.

A variety of personal factors may also serve to affect any relationship between satisfaction and absence. Many people feel that it is wrong to accept pay without work (equity theory) or to let others down capriciously. Another factor constraining people from absenting themselves unnecessarily is that individuals are likely to feel that it is not expedient to acquire a reputation for poor attendance, because of the effect on future references when applying for other jobs. Indeed, it might well lead to job termination through sacking.

It would appear, therefore, that individuals may feel a commitment to work for a variety of reasons and these reasons may be a far better predictor of absence behaviour than satisfaction with work. In general terms, an individual who is dissatisfied with his job may attend because the rewards for attendance are not purely in terms of satisfaction with the job, but are to do with factors discussed above. On the other hand, someone satisfied with his job may, on occasions, absent himself if he feels no moral constraints and the attractions off the job are temporarily more attractive than those on it.

In conclusion, it appears quite clear that, as with the relationship between satisfaction and productivity, the relationship between satisfaction and absence is complex and unclear. Again, however, it might be that some of the conclusions of Nicholson *et al.*, and Ilgen and Hollenbach, are perhaps too gloomy. There are a number of studies which do show a relationship. The methodological defects from which they suffer means that they must be treated with some caution, yet it might be rash to discount their findings completely.

What present research has undoubtedly shown is that many other factors, unrelated to job satisfaction, may also be operating. As Ilgen and Hollenbach note:

> The lack of support for the position that job satisfaction causes absenteeism does not imply that absence behaviour is any less important or less researchable. It does imply that a more efficacious approach to it must be undertaken than merely to correlate it with satisfaction measures. The focus of an organisation interested in absenteeism behaviour must be on these factors within the organisation which influence the provision of valued rewards (or sanctions) for attendance behaviour. The concern with job satisfaction is only an indirect one. Whether or not job satisfaction correlates with absenteeism depends on whether they share a common third partner – the attainment of valued rewards.

JOB SATISFACTION AND TURNOVER

The evidence concerning the relationship between job satisfaction and employee turnover appears far more conclusive than does that of satisfaction and absence. Porter and Steers, for example, examined fifteen studies published between 1955 and 1972, and found a positive relationship in all but one. A typical study is that of Hulin (1966), who examined the relationship between satisfaction and turnover in a group of female clerical workers. He compared those who left the company and those who stayed over a twelve-month period, on a number of dimensions, including their scores on a job satisfaction scale which had previously been administered. The results indicated that the leavers had substantially lower levels of job satisfaction before leaving the organisation than did those who stayed. Subsequently, the company introduced changes in salary and promotion with the effect of increasing satisfaction and reducing turnover from 30 per cent to 12 per cent. Again, however, those who did leave were more dissatisfied than those who stayed.

The next question which arises is why dissatisfaction leads to job change and which job factors are important in making an individual change his job? Porter and Steers consider a number of factors, all of which appear to have a significant effect on precipitating resignation. The first of these is pay and promotion, with substantial evidence to suggest that low pay and lack of promotion opportunity can be a major cause of resignation. However, the problem appears to be not only one of the actual level of pay but also perceived equitable level of pay. The case is similar with regard to promotion procedures, which for some occupations appear to be a major cause of dissatisfaction because of lack of perceived equitability in their administration.

Other factors which Porter and Steers consider in relation to satisfaction and turnover include job content, supervision and personality factors. Of the job content factors, task repetitiveness has been shown to be related to employee turnover in a number of studies, although a study by Kilbridge (1951) failed to find any relationship. Kilbridge argues that factors such as the payments system and group pressure have a greater impact on turnover than task repetitiveness and, as was noted in Chapter 3, some individuals prefer simple tasks to complex ones. Autonomy (that is, the extent of control over one's own work) has been shown to be related to turnover in a number of studies but, again, the relationship is not significant.

As far as the relationship between supervision and turnover is concerned, a number of studies have shown the relationship between considerate leadership (supervision) and employee turnover. However, two studies found that considerate supervision is only effective in reducing turnover up to a point. Beyond a certain point other factors start to take over as being important in the decision to withdraw from the job.

Related to the question of social support from the supervisor is the question of social support from one's peers. Here, a number of studies have demonstrated a relationship between degree of social interaction with one's peers and turnover. Porter and Steers argue again, however, that it is not so much social interaction which affects turnover, but whether the individual's expectations regarding social interaction on the job situation are met.

Finally, the question of individual factors should be considered as it is frequently held that certain individuals are 'turnover prone'. One aspect is whether the person has chosen the right job in terms of his vocational interests. There is evidence that those who regard their job as being in line with their vocational interests are less likely to leave than others. Thus, employees who have no clear idea of where their vocational interests lie may well be more turnover prone than those with clear ideas. As far as personality factors are concerned, Porter and Steers conclude that

> a tendency exists for employees manifesting very high degrees of anxiety, emotional insecurity, aggression, self-confidence, and ambition, to leave the organisation at a higher rate than employees possessing such traits in a more moderate degree.

Such traits may or may not be related to perceived job satisfaction. To the extent that they are not related, they will, of course, further reduce the relationship found between job satisfaction and turnover.

Apart from personality, then, a number of factors such as job content, supervision, pay and peer relationships affect turnover. Given the relationship between overall satisfaction and turnover, one would, of course, expect such factors as job content to be related to turnover as they have been shown to be related to overall job satisfaction. Yet as Porter and Steers argue, it is not so much the presence or absence of factors *per se* which is related to turnover, it is the extent to which expectations concerning these factors are met on the job. Despite reservations of workers such as

Locke (1976) concerning the importance of expectations in job satisfaction (see Chapter 2), a number of studies have examined the effects on job turnover of giving job applicants realistic information and hence realistic expectations concerning their jobs. Making expectations realistic is likely to have positive effects on turnover for two reasons. Firstly, if it is clear to an individual that what he values from a job will not be met, then he will not join the organisation in the first place. Secondly, those who do join will, perhaps, pay more attention to the values which can be fulfilled and which they may not have realised were present on the job. These values then will act as compensation for others which cannot be fulfilled. Porter and Steers quote two unpublished studies in which altered individual expectations were related to lower job turnover, a finding supported by Scott (1972). However, no evidence is presented on whether changes took place in what was valued on the job, so that it is possible that lower turnover is due to changes in values rather than expectations (see Chapter 2). This, of course, is an academic point. The question of practical significance is whether or not changes in initial job knowledge might affect future turnover. The answer would appear to be 'yes'.

There has recently been an attempt to assess the economic effects of job turnover; Mirvis and Lawler (1977) examined the relationship between job attitudes, absence and turnover of bank tellers. The correlation between employee attitudes and turnover was relatively low (about -0.20), although significant. As the cost of one resignation, in terms of hiring and training, is estimated to be $2522.03, a relatively small reduction in the incidence of turnover could have a marked effect on costs. The relationship between satisfaction and absenteeism was very high (-0.81), although the investigators point to a number of reasons why this particular figure should be treated with caution. The cost of an absence in the organisation studied was $66.45, so again, the economic implications are considerable. The results of the study must be treated with even greater caution than normal in view of the failure of a number of other studies to find any relationship between job satisfaction and absence. As in many other studies, no relationship was found between absence and turnover, which suggests that rather different causes of each behaviour are operating in this particular group. On the basis of statistical analysis, Mirvis and Lawler estimate that to increase the job satisfaction of the group by half a standard deviation would reduce costs by $17 664. This implies that in theory, if each individual's job satisfaction were to be increased to its maximum, the cost of reduction would be $125 160.

Mirvis and Lawler argue that the type of analysis which they use enables managers to assess the implications of improving job satisfaction in financial terms. Yet one must be cautious about this approach. It has been seen how changes in job satisfaction are not necessarily accompanied by changes in motivation and productivity. Increasing rewards, therefore, although it may improve job satisfaction and reduce turnover and absence, could conceivably reduce *profits* by costing more than savings arising from improvement in turnover and absence. For example, a $10 a week rise in pay would cost $86 200 for this group; it is not obvious that satisfaction would increase sufficiently to make this move worthwhile. Similarly, structural alterations in the job (job enrichment) might cost more than savings arising through reduced turnover. Finally, as has been suggested earlier, some rewards, such as increasing job security, might increase job satisfaction and at the same time increase absence behaviour. Mirvis and Lawler, too, admit limitations in their approach. For example, estimates of turnover in times of high unemployment are likely to be misleading when applied to times of low unemployment. Furthermore, they caution the reader against generalising the results by applying them to other organisations where, of course, the costs of absence and turnover will be entirely different, with different cost benefits.

In summary, therefore, the results suggest that there exists a relationship between job satisfaction and employee turnover, although the magnitude of the relationship is not necessarily very large. This is because a large number of factors, not necessarily connected with the job, will result in dissatisfied individuals continuing employment. Conversely of course, some satisfied individuals may change their employment because of promotion, ambition, and of course, external personal reasons. Many facets of job satisfaction have been shown to relate to turnover, including job content, supervisory practice, pay and social relationships.

JOB SATISFACTION AND COUNTER-PRODUCTIVE BEHAVIOUR

In considering the economic implications of job satisfaction, one area of cost considered by Mirvis and Lawler is that of counter-productive behaviour. Assumptions are not infrequently made that in industry job dissatisfaction is related to a high incidence of counter-productive behaviour, such as sabotage. Mangoine and Quinn (1975) have recently called into question some of the 'scaring' statistics produced. They argue that many reports refer only to alarming incidents and suggest that many reports fail to present any adequate statistics on the subject. Their own study involved a national sample of 1327 wage-earners and salaried workers and demonstrated a significant relationship between expressed job satisfaction and self reports of counter-productive behaviour of different kinds. Their results are given in Table 1. As can be seen, the correlations are not large, but many are statistically significant, indicating that job dissatisfaction can have economic effects over and above those of turnover and absence.

Counter-productive behaviour involves much more than actual sabotage; it can involve causing trouble, doing work badly on purpose, and theft. Mars (1977) emphasises the importance of 'fiddling' employers in order to obtain equitable rewards. Possibly those who undertake such 'fiddling' are more dissatisfied with the job, at least in terms of the financial rewards, than those in other occupations. Of course, one must be careful of generalisations, as opportunity to thieve will vary from occupation to occupation, as will the social consequences of being caught. On

TABLE 1 Correlations Between Job Satisfaction, and Counter-productive
Behaviour and Drug Use at Work

	Men's ages		Women's ages	
Indicator of counter-productive behaviour and drug use	16–29 years (*n* = 277)	≥ 30 years (*n* = 581)	16–29 years (*n* = 172)	≥ 30 years (*n* = 285)
Spread rumours or gossip to cause trouble at work	−.15*	−.14**	−.10	−.10
Did work badly or incorrectly on purpose	−.07	−.19**	.09	−.12*
Stole merchandise or equipment from employer	.03	−.12**	−.06	.00
Damaged employer's property, equipment, or product accidently, but did not report it	−.04	−.07	.02	−.06
Damaged employer's property, equipment, or product on purpose	−.11	−.13**	.02	.01
Index of counter-productive behaviour	−.09	−.18**	.02	−.07
Used drugs or chemicals (except vitamins or aspirin) to help get through the work day	−.04	−.12**	.01	−.08

Note. Pearson product-moment correlations (*r*) were used.
* $p < .05$.
** $p < .01$.

(From Mangoine, T. W. and Quinn, R. P. 'Job satisfaction, counter-productive behaviour, and drug use at work,' *J. Applied Psychology* (1975) 60, 114–16.© 1975 by the American Psychological Association. Reprinted by permission.)

the other hand, Mars' work has shown that 'fiddling' is extremely wide-spread, and, in some cases, so institutionalised that it might not be reported as theft by respondents.

An interesting finding of Mangoine and Quinn was that the relationship between job satisfaction and counter-productive behaviour held only for those over thirty years of age. This must not be interpreted as meaning that counter-productive behaviour is greater amongst men over thirty. On the contrary, men under thirty were more inclined to take part in such behaviour. However, it was only for men over thirty that this kind of behaviour was related to job satisfaction. Perhaps family responsibilities make men, as they get older, less likely to indulge in counter-productive behaviour, unless they feel a sense of grievance on the job.

One important aspect of counter-productive behaviour is the propensity to strike. Common sense would suggest that those most dissatisfied are those most likely to strike. Certainly there is evidence that certain groups, such as car workers, have a greater record of striking than do other groups and that such strike-prone industries are generally of the conveyor belt technology kind. However, individuals may be job satisfied in general but dissatisfied about one aspect, such as pay, and this alone might induce a strike.

JOB SATISFACTION AND THE INDIVIDUAL

So far, the effects of job satisfaction have been considered in terms of their potential economic effects. However, another major reason for studying job satisfaction is its effects on the individual's life. After all, most individuals spend a substantial part of their lives in work situations and so how they are affected in terms of personal wellbeing is of central importance in its own right, whatever the economic effects. At least two questions might be posed. Firstly, how do job satisfaction and dissatisfaction affect physical and mental health and secondly, how do they affect satisfaction with other aspects of the individual's life? These will be considered in turn.

Job satisfaction and physical health

A number of studies have suggested that job satisfaction can have major effects on physical wellbeing. If true, this would not be a surprising finding. It is reasonable to suppose that job dissatisfaction, in an extreme form, causes stress and stress is clearly related to a number of physical illnesses such as heart disease and peptic ulcers. Yet as with other areas of job satisfaction, it would be surprising if the relationship between job dissatisfaction and physical illness was high. Many individuals are stressed in their jobs and in their lives for reasons which have nothing to do with job satisfaction. The business executive, for example, may be under constant pressure to make important decisions but may well enjoy doing so. Doctors are often under enormous pressure when they are daily making life-saving decisions about large numbers of individuals, yet doctors, for the most part, are devoted to their profession. Furthermore, not only might 'on the job' stress be enjoyable, stress from other areas of life, such as family, might serve to mask any major effect of job dissatisfaction on illness.

Despite the limitations outlined above, there is some evidence for a relationship between job dissatisfaction and physical illness. Palmore, (1969), for example, found that work satisfaction was the single best predictor of longevity with a correlation of 0·26, an even better predictor than tobacco use. However, the study was of a limited sample of 268 individuals. Reviewing the literature, Jenkins (1971) cites some further studies which have found a relationship between heart disease and job dissatisfaction. As he points out, however, it is possible that those most prone to heart disease are more likely to complain about their working environment. Job involvement, as well as job satisfaction, is reported as being a critical factor in heart disease, with the incidence of heart attacks increasing very significantly following a setback at work.

In a recent review of occupational sources of stress, Cooper and Marshall (1976) support the view that stress at work is related to heart disease and also to mental ill health. In particular, stress produced by assembly lines, poor supervisory practices and lack of a fulfilling job all appear to be related to an increased incidence of heart disease. Like earlier reviewers, however, Cooper and Marshall note the methodological inadequacies of many of the studies. Whilst, therefore, studies give some support for the view that physical illness can be caused by job dissatisfaction, on the basis of present knowledge it would be unwise to presume that this was more important than a variety of physical causes such as smoking, lack of exercise and a sedentary job, or even genetic and personality predisposition. As Locke (1976) notes, however, the field is fascinating and it would be foolish to ignore the way the research findings are pointing.

Job satisfaction and mental health

Perhaps the most influential voice in drawing attention to the effects of job dissatisfaction on mental health has been that of Kornhauser (1965), who defines and measures mental health on a number of dimensions, including self-esteem, anxiety, hostility, sociability and life satisfaction. On the basis of his studies he concludes that gratifications and deprivations experienced in work and expressed in job dissatisfaction are important determinants of workers' mental health.

Hoppock (1935) and Ferguson (1973) have also noted a relationship between job satisfaction and mental health. Hoppock found that the least job-satisfied teachers in his sample could be distinguished from the most satisfied in terms of emotional maladaptation, as evidenced by their responses to such questions as 'Do you often feel just miserable?' or 'Do you often feel lonesome when you are with other people?'

Ferguson's results indicated that telegraphists diagnosed as neurotic in a medical examination most commonly attributed their symptoms to the adverse work environment, including a boring job. It is interesting to note that in Kornhauser's study the strongest relationship was between mental health and the chance to use abilities. Kornhauser notes that many studies have shown that the lower the level of job, the more likely it is that the worker will have mental health problems.

Reviewing the literature, Kasl (1973) points out that whilst few studies disagree with such findings, the interpretations are open to doubt. The main problem is that it is difficult to isolate low level work from other problems in the environment which might be associated with it and which cause stress. For example, low level work is normally associated with low levels of pay, poor living conditions, family stress and so on. Furthermore, it is possible that individuals with mental health problems will find it difficult to keep higher level jobs and will gravitate downwards. Kasl also points out that when relationships are found between job level, mental health and job satisfaction, those relationships are invariably of a low magnitude. Finally, as Kasl notes, there are a number of important exceptions to the job level–mental health relationship. Clerical workers, for example, who have relatively high level jobs, have a poor record of mental health.

A number of other investigators have also questioned the degree to which job satisfaction is an important factor in mental health. Orpen (1974), for example, has shown that the relationship between expressed job satisfaction and mental health is inflated because of socially desirable responses to both questionnaires. Thus people may say they are job-satisfied when they are not and may cover up mental health problems because of fears concerning what others might think. When the effects are taken into account, the relationship is very small. One might therefore take issue with Kornhauser's view that mental health problems are an important consequence of job dissatisfaction in quantitative terms at least, although for the individuals concerned they are obviously of considerable importance. On the basis of the present evidence, however, one must agree with Kasl, who concludes that

> The safest conclusion from the existing evidence is that, given the relatively weak association between job satisfaction and other indices of mental health, various aspects of the work environment could have a strong impact on job satisfaction without having much impact on symptoms or other areas of satisfaction (p. 514).

Why job satisfaction and mental health are not strongly related is, of course, an important question to which there is probably no one answer. Various writers have argued that the main reason is that most people are so resilient that even in adversity they can cope adequately. Certainly it is likely that those who are extremely unhappy in a job will move to another which is more in line with their needs, whilst those staying will be likely to find compensation in their job situation which may not be related to the job itself, such as in social relationships. Thus, the job satisfaction–mental health relationship is low because the extremes of job satisfaction which might cause mental ill health are not normally reached.

As Warr and Wall point out, there are two aspects of mental health: mental ill health and positive wellbeing. Positive wellbeing, of course, goes beyond mere existence implied by negative concepts of health to actually deriving fulfilment from life. Whilst there might be little solid evidence that a poor working situation will lead to large numbers of individuals suffering from mental illness, the evidence discussed in Chapter 3 shows quite clearly that many jobs do not provide much opportunity for the individual to add to his psychological wellbeing. Boring, dull, repetitive jobs may be such that individuals can adapt to the situation, but writers such as Herzberg (1966) and Warr and Wall (1975) argue that men at work can reasonably ask more of life. Job redesign, job enlargement and job enrichment all have the aim of improving the mental health of the individual by allowing for psychological growth on the job. Certainly, there appears to be considerable room for improvement in job design in relation to mental health. Kornhauser, for example, found that those in mechanically paced production line operations had a worse record of mental health than those in routine jobs, which, however, were not mechanically paced.

In conclusion, therefore, it appears that mental health is related to job satisfaction but that the relationship is of a low order. This might be because individuals are resilient to poor working conditions and will seek their satisfaction from aspects of their job other than work itself. That the relationship between job satisfaction and mental health is low should not disguise the fact that many individuals in low level jobs fail to derive positive mental health from their work. Furthermore, whilst statistically unimportant, the effect of mental illness derived from job dissatisfaction on any one individual is disastrous in its effects on feelings of self-esteem, self-confidence and on life satisfaction in general. For a manager to ignore the problem because it is statistically unimportant would be inhuman.

Job satisfaction and life satisfaction

Satisfaction with life in general was one of the indices of mental health investigated by Kornhauser and has also been previously considered by Hoppock (1935). He noted that dissatisfied teachers came from unhappy home backgrounds. This leads to the suggestion that there exist some individuals who are basically happy and some who are basically unhappy as a result of their life experiences. Job dissatisfaction, therefore, may occur where individuals predisposed to being unhappy are placed in practically any job situation.

Two distinct theories of the relationship between job and life satisfaction have been proposed; the *compensation theory* which argues that, in order to compensate for dissatisfaction at work, one derives greater satisfaction with the other aspects of life, and the *spillover theory* which argues that unhappiness at work is likely to affect one's whole life. The compensation theory would therefore predict a negative correlation between job and life satisfaction whereas the spillover theory would predict a positive correlation.

From studies which have investigated the problem, the spillover theory is almost universally supported. Kornhauser (1965), for example, found those unhappy in their jobs tended to be unhappy with life in general. Of course, the relationship between job and life satisfaction is a two-way process and it is just as possible that satisfaction with life in general affects satisfaction with the job, so that the causal aspect of the relationship is unclear.

Iris and Barrett (1972) carried out a study which succeeded in showing that job satisfaction can act to affect life satisfaction. They compared the job and life satisfaction of two groups of foremen from two different departments in a chemical firm. One group had been identified by the management as a 'problem' group in terms of job performance whereas the other group were not considered as problematic. There was no suggestion that allocation to these groups was on the lines of life satisfaction measures.

The two groups were given the Job Descriptive Index in order to measure job satisfaction in five areas, together with a 'satisfaction with life' questionnaire. Iris and Barrett found that the foremen from the 'problem' group had lower job satisfaction in all five areas examined and lower life satisfaction. As the foremen were differentiated in terms of their job rather than in terms of individual differences when they entered employment, the results are a clear indication that the jobs produced dissatisfaction which extended beyond the work situation. Iris and Barrett also examined the pattern of relationships between job factor importance and life satisfaction. They found that those who were dissatisfied with other aspects of life than their jobs were those who regarded dissatisfying aspects of their jobs as important. The investigators conclude that the lack of job involvement is a healthy response where there is dissatisfaction. By reducing the importance of a dissatisfying aspect of a job, the individual is able to defend his self-esteem.

It must be noted, however, that on the basis of one study, it is not possible to exclude the possibility that the compensation theory can operate in some situations for some individuals. Faunce and Dubin (1975), for example, argue that the two possibilities are not mutually exclusive. They point to work which shows young, alienated workers developing a self-investment which was an alternative to investment in work because they did not see work as providing opportunities for fulfilment (see Goldthorpe *et al.*, 1968). Faunce and Dubin suggest that, for healthy adjustment, withdrawal of investment in work before retiral is desirable.

Clearly the relationship between job and life satisfaction is complex, depending on personality factors, the job and personal circumstances. When relationships do exist, this might be because a cheerful individual will enjoy both work and other life factors where a more morose individual would complain about both. The extent to which a job gives the potential for job involvement will affect the amount of personal investment which, to some extent, will determine the effect of job dissatisfaction on life satisfaction. A further moderating factor is that a poor job is likely to be associated with poor pay and hence poor social conditions. For all of these reasons, a straightforward interpretation of the relationship between life and job satisfaction is impossible. It is, however, possible to say, on the basis of the study by Iris and Barrett, that evidence exists to suggest that job satisfaction can influence felt life satisfaction.

SUMMARY

It is quite clear that, however much social scientists would wish job satisfaction to affect aspects of economic importance, the research findings have been somewhat unimpressive. At present there is little conclusive evidence that job satisfaction affects productivity at all and indeed, the more popular current theory suggests that productivity affects job satisfaction. It must be borne in mind, however, that this theory too, has little evidence to support it. All that exists in fact is a body of research findings which show inconsistent and usually low correlations between satisfaction and productivity. On the other hand, the results do suggest that where the needs of individuals are taken into account, the relationship between satisfaction and productivity is sometimes significant. Whatever the relationship between productivity and satisfaction, it is complex and incompletely understood at present. The hope must be that the variables affecting the relationship will be isolated in future work so that conditions which support the productivity–satisfaction relationship can be specified and utilised by managers.

The satisfaction–absence relationship is little clearer than that of the satisfaction–productivity relationship. Whilst a number of studies have reported a relationship, the analysis of Nicholson *et al.* throws the validity of any general conclusion into doubt. At present, it is safest to conclude that a satisfaction – absence relationship may exist, that research findings have been inconsistent and that the magnitude of any relationship is likely to be small.

The relationship between absence and turnover is also unclear, although the relationship between satisfaction and turnover does seem to be reasonably well established. Even here, however, a large number of factors are important – for example, the possibility of alternative employment – so that the magnitude of the relationship varies considerably from study to study.

A final economic variable, counter-productive behaviour, has also been shown to have a small, although significant relationship with job satisfaction, at least in older individuals. There is little systematic published material in this area, however, so that the real economic effects of job satisfaction in relation to this factor remain in doubt.

Whilst the tentative conclusions regarding the effects of overall job satisfaction are disappointing for those wishing to apply knowledge from social science to the real world, it must not be forgotten that one is dealing with extremely complex behaviour. Inconsistencies in findings are bound to exist in profusion where cultural, personality and organisational factors all vary and where few researchers use the same instruments to measure the phenomena under investigation. The present state of confusion is indeed healthy if it shows the manager just how complex the problems are and forestalls any attempt to provide simple prescriptions for solving human relations and organisational problems on a 'once and for all' basis. On the other hand, there is sufficient evidence to suggest that certain kinds of job characteristics are related to facets of job satisfaction and productivity and these are considered in the next chapter.

7 Job Satisfaction and Job Design

The problem of redesigning jobs to give individuals greater job satisfaction has received considerable attention in recent years. A large number of studies have been published which have shown changes in job satisfaction as a result of changes in the way in which the work is organised, e.g. Trist and Bamforth (Chapter 4). The important question, however, is not so much whether job satisfaction can be improved, but whether it can be improved in the context of increased organisational efficiency. After all, most organisations could increase job satisfaction by giving their workers an unconditional £20 per week pay rise, but such a step would probably lead to bankruptcy. In order to be worthwhile, changes in job design must be shown to have effects which justify themselves in economic ways, as well as in terms of increased job satisfaction, although of course increased productivity is not the only criterion of economic improvement. In addition to increased productivity and better quality of production, reductions in employee absence, turnover or counter-productive behaviour might all be of sufficient economic importance to justify job redesign. On the other hand, even if productivity is increased it may not be economically justified if the cost of new equipment is, say, ten million pounds and only two extra cars per week are produced. The important question then is whether job satisfaction can be improved in the context of increased profitability.

Historically, changes in job design were aimed at improving productivity with little or no thought given to job satisfaction. Taylor's (1911) approach to scientific management involved the use of financial incentives and technological changes in order to improve productivity. The limitations of this approach were exposed by the Hawthorne studies which showed the importance of social factors in limiting productivity in the bank wiring room experiment. Thereafter, the 'Human Relations' school emphasised the importance of designing jobs bearing in mind the importance of human relationships at work. More recently, the emphasis on job redesign has changed. The job itself is seen as the important determinant of job satisfaction and current approaches to job redesign concentrate on this aspect of the work situation.

THE NATURE OF JOB REDESIGN

Various investigators have distinguished between different kinds of 'actual job' redesign. At its simplest, job redesign might involve only job rotation, where individuals change actual jobs which they are doing from day to day or from week to week. For example, there might be five jobs carried out in a particular department using a job rotation scheme. On Monday, the individual will begin doing job 1 and, by Friday, will be on job 5. On the following Monday he starts off with job 1 again, and so on. The idea behind job rotation is that it reduces the repetitive nature of the job and hence reduces boredom. Job rotation has a large number of critics, however. Herzberg (1968), for example, believes that job rotation merely gives the individual more boring jobs without increasing the potential for development and growth. Another objection to job rotation is that it can disrupt the social relationships which the individual establishes in the work situation and which, for so many people in low level jobs, are an important source of job satisfaction. This may be true even where a group as a whole is moved from job to job, if the technical arrangements involved different patterns of interaction. A further conflicting factor in job rotation is that it requires training on new jobs, with a possible loss of income for the individual until his skill improves. Nevertheless, it may be the case that, in certain situations, job rotation is desirable. This is particularly true where individuals themselves wish for job rotation or where other kinds of job redesign are not practicable. Volvo, for example, is one organisation where job rotation is sometimes included as part of job redesign (Gyllenhammer, 1977), although it is not thought to be effective in isolation from other job design changes.

✳ A second kind of job redesign is that of horizontal job enlargement. This takes place when a number of operations are added to the job that the individual is expected to perform. For example, the new job might require an increase in the number of units to be tightened or holes to be drilled or perhaps require both holes to be drilled and units to be tightened rather than just performing one of the operations. The logic behind horizontal job enlargement is that, by increasing the complexity of the job, one is increasing the challenge to the individual and thus his job satisfaction. Herzberg and others have argued, however, that increasing the number of boring and unskilled acts is not of itself likely to add very much to the challenge of the job or to the personal development of the individual. On the other hand, it should be pointed out that Walker and Guest (1952) found the greater the number of operations an individual performed, the greater was his job satisfaction.

✴Most writers on job enlargement, however, are concerned with redesigning jobs through job enrichment (otherwise known as vertical job enlargement), so that self-actualisation and psychological growth are possible. Such redesigned jobs aim to go beyond merely increasing job satisfaction, which might be attained by increasing lower order rewards, to allow the individual to apply skill to the performance of his job and thus satisfy his higher order needs. As was seen in Chapter 3, this implies that the individual becomes responsible for making choices between alternatives, and this in turn means that he must take responsibility for decisions concerning how his job should be done. Job enrichment, therefore, not only involves horizontal job enlargement in the sense of increasing the complexity and variety of the task to be done, but also involves giving the job meaning and challenge. Furthermore, by requiring the application of skill and judgement, changes in supervisory practices from authoritarian to participative are called for. Indeed, some writers have argued that it is best to abandon supervision in favour of autonomous work-groups who monitor their own performance. Finally, if the individual is to be able to develop his skills, he must have feedback from his superiors as to how well he is progressing. It is argued that only by changing the four core aspects of the job (task autonomy, variety, identity and feedback) is it likely that the individual will be able to develop psychologically on the job.

An example of what job enrichment involves is given by Locke, Sirota and Wolfson (1976). They reported a project designed to enrich the jobs of clerical workers in a Government Agency. They wrote of one group:

> Clerks were allowed to decide for themselves what needed to be done with certain types of files. Instruction forms formerly filled out by another unit were eliminated. When work was completed, they decided themselves where it should be sent rather than going to their supervisors. If search material could not be found, they decided themselves what the next step should be rather than being told. Clerks were allotted time to various tasks based on what needed to be done, rather than on what was assigned to them. They kept their own time records. On a rotational basis, one member was assigned to the job of unit captain whose job it was to screen incoming work, compile unit time records, despatch outgoing work and the like. The captain could also make phone calls directly to other units regarding problem files rather than have the superior do it. Eventually all employees could make such calls themselves at any time. This unit also called meetings with other units to go over common problems related to filing.

Locke *et al.* regard such changes as involving a substantial increase in meaningfulness and autonomy and slight changes in feedback and variety of task.

Unlike many earlier studies of job enrichment, the experiment of Locke *et al.* is one which can be regarded as well-designed. It incorporates control groups, uses appropriate measures of job attitude and analyses the results in statistical terms. As was noted above, the experiment involved considerable design changes, which can be regarded as enriching the job. The results showed increases in productivity, improved attendance and turnover figures, but no improvement in job satisfaction. Locke *et al.* suggest that productivity improved, not because of increased satisfaction brought about by job design changes but because the job design changes themselves improved the efficiency of the job by, for example, improving manpower utilisation.

The failure to find changes in job attitudes is perhaps the most interesting part of the study. The investigators questioned the clerical workers involved and found that disappointment was created by the failure of management to reward them with improved pay for their improved performance. Locke *et al.* argue that this shows the clerical workers to be motivated basically by extrinsic rewards: although work was important, it took second place to financial returns.

Whilst such an interpretation is quite possible, the most intrinsically motivated individual is likely to become upset if he feels exploited and inequitably treated by his employers. This may be the case in Locke *et al.*'s study, given that increased productivity was not financially rewarded. In such a situation, individuals may well feel that job redesign is a management tool to increase productivity without increasing pay. As Locke *et al.* point out, job enrichment schemes must pay attention to tangible rewards as well as to improvements in the intrinsic aspects of the job. Indeed, as was noted before, financial reward may well operate as a means of recognition of increased value to the organisation.

Contrary to the findings of Locke *et al.*, Alderfer (1969) reports a study which shows increased satisfaction with job enrichment. He studied a manufacturing plant which used a continuous processing system, the type of organisation often claimed to be difficult to enrich. This job enrichment programme had two important features. First, those individuals taking part in the job enrichment programme were carefully selected as being the best workers. Second, those on the job enrichment programme were paid more than those whose jobs were not enriched. The enrichment aspects of the job involved operating new and complex machinery, and the workers were asked to undertake a number of additional duties including accounting, personnel work and scheduling.

Not surprisingly, Alderfer reports an increase in satisfaction with pay and with the work itself. To this extent, the job enrichment programme seems successful in improving the quality of working life. On the other hand, relationships with superiors deteriorated as a result of the enrichment programme. This finding has been reported elsewhere and it has been suggested that increasing the scope of the workers' jobs can threaten the role and status of supervisors by taking from them important aspects of their work. Job enrichment, therefore, can be a mixed blessing in which one man's job enrichment is another man's job impoverishment.

Other studies also suggest that human relationships can be adversely affected by job enrichment. Lawler, Hackman and Kaufmann (1973), for example, found that both peer and superior-subordinate relationships were beset with problems after a job enrichment programme, and in reviewing studies on job enrichment, Alderfer (1976) concludes that it is probably the rare job enrichment experiment that does not imply relationship changes as well as job changes. In one study, for example, women workers were given control over the speed of their production line. As a consequence, pay and job satisfaction increased. However, other workers became upset at these changes and pressure was brought to bear to stop the experiment. As many researchers have noted, one cannot make changes in one aspect of an organisation without considering the repercussions on other parts, however successful the changes are.

Like many studies on job enrichment, Alderfer's study suffers from a number of limitations. As Alderfer points out, it is hardly surprising that satisfaction with pay increased – the enriched group was being paid more! On the other hand, as was noted above, a failure to pay individuals more might lead to feelings of inequity, particularly if productivity is improved. The second problem was that those selected for the enrichment programme were not selected at random, but were the 'best' blue collar workers. Thus a comparison with other groups is not reasonable. As was noted in previous chapters, however, not every individual has the inclination to be involved in acquiring greater skills. Furthermore, from an organisational point of view, it does seem reasonable to judge the success of a scheme when the most appropriate people are chosen for the job, rather than selecting individuals at random. No football manager would judge a new technique for scoring goals by having his least skilled players operating it.

Another well-known study which shows positive effects of job enrichment is that of Paul, Robertson and Herzberg (1969). This study investigated the effects of job content changes. To do this, 'hygiene factors' were held constant. Among the group whose jobs were enriched were sales representatives, experimental officers, design engineers and factory supervisors. The enrichment of the sales representatives' jobs involved giving more responsibility for decision-making concerning sales. As they were paid a salary, there was no financial inducement to sell more. The result of the experiment showed that job satisfaction and productivity increased as a result of the job enrichment programme. The experimental groups *increased* sales by 19 per cent whereas a control group reduced sales by 5 per cent. The difference is reported as being statistically significant. As far as job satisfaction was concerned, the control group did not improve but the enriched group improved by 11 per cent. Unfortunately, it is not possible to say whether or not this is statistically significant.

At first sight there would appear to be a contradiction between the findings of Locke *et al.* and Paul *et al.* on the need for financial incentives. However, initial job satisfaction for those workers investigated by Paul *et al.* was high whereas this was not the case in the Locke *et al.* study. In a situation where individuals feel that they are equitably treated in terms of their job, it may well be that financial incentives need not be tied to increased output. On the other hand, it may be as Locke *et al.* suggest, that certain individuals value financial incentive highly and become dissatisfied if increased performance is not linked to increased payment. Without knowing a great deal more about the background of the individuals in both studies, little can be made of the differences in findings. As far as the other groups studied by Paul *et al.* are concerned, the results showed similar improvements to those of the salesmen. For example, the job satisfaction of the design engineers increased by up to 21 per cent for the enriched group with no improvement in the control group. As Warr and Wall point out, however, all the reported studies by Paul *et al.* are limited in the conclusions which can be drawn, as critical information is missing.

Perhaps the most famous job enrichment study is that carried out at the American Telephone and Telegraph Company (A T & T) and reported by Ford (1969). Based on Herzberg's theories, the investigators began by enriching the jobs of girls who answered letters of complaint in the treasury department. The enrichment procedures involved, amongst other things, having the girls sign their own names rather than refer to supervisors, having the girls deal with difficult as well as easy assignments and reducing the frequency of supervisory checks from 100 per cent to 10 per cent.

Ford reports that job satisfaction, turnover, attendance, quantity and quality of the production improved although clear statistical evidence is missing. Nevertheless, the success was felt to be great enough to proceed with a further nineteen job enrichment schemes in departments such as engineering and trafffic. Improvements in satisfaction and productivity were again reported although the magnitude of the improvement was not necessarily as large as in the first study.

It is often argued that job enrichment is applicable only to reasonably high level jobs where rigid technology does not preclude job redesign. A study by Sirota and Wolfson (1972) shows how a job rigidly determined by technology can be enriched when there is a desire for change. One enrichment programme, for example, involved changing the jobs of men tending silicon wafer slicing machines in an electronics factory. Rather than being mere machine-minders, the men were given training in maintenance, and were given authority to change slicing blades when they thought it appropriate. They were also given daily feedback on their performance. As a result of the changes made, maintenance costs fell to almost zero, production increased, and the attitude of employees improved. Furthermore, the satisfaction of the maintenance men also increased as they were free to concentrate on more complex maintenance work. Whilst Sirota and Wolfson's report certainly points to the advantages of job redesign, even in rigid technological situations, it must be admitted that no adequate statistical information is provided. The same comments can be made of Gyllenhammer's (1977) account of job redesign in the Volvo car assembly lines. Here too, jobs in a rigid technological system have been redesigned to allow individuals to use their skills in tackling a complete car assembly job in work teams, rather than by small routine jobs on the assembly line. As with Sirota and Wolfson's study, job redesign in the Volvo plant appears to be accompanied by increased productivity and job satisfaction.

A number of attempts have been made to assess the considerable number of studies on job enrichment. Several reviewers have pointed out that many, if not all, of the studies have considerable limitations. Warr and Wall (1975), for example, suggest that much of the evidence for improved satisfaction is based on studies whose general standard of experimental design is poor.

A first criticism which is often levelled is that a large number of changes are made simultaneously, making it difficult to be sure that improvements are due to job redesign. For example, in many studies, increased responsibility is accompanied by increased payment, so that improved job satisfaction might be due to either of these factors.

A second criticism often made against many studies is that no adequate control group is used with which to compare the performance of the enriched group. This point was noted when discussing the Alderfer (1969) study, where, for example, no attempt was made to match the enriched and unenriched groups, in terms of capacities and skills.

Such criticisms raise fundamental questions about the scientific criteria which should be applied when assessing the findings of job enrichment studies. In many cases, the practicalities of life make it impossible to carry out controlled laboratory experiments. Indeed, some writers such as Katzell and Yankelovich (1975) have argued that only by making a large number of simultaneous changes in the jobs is it possible to induce major changes in satisfaction and productivity. It does not matter, therefore, if it is impossible to isolate the causal factors involved in change in any one study, as long as it works. Similarly, for the criticism concerning inadequate controls: if there are improvements following job enrichment after selecting the best workers, then does it matter in practical terms that the exact nature of the improvement cannot be determined?

Whilst appeals to practical difficulties in experimental design might be justified for the kind of problem discussed above, the same cannot be said of the inadequacy of statistical evidence found in the great majority of studies. Until more statistical evidence is forthcoming, critics are entitled to question the validity of conclusions based on job enrichment studies. Nevertheless, in spite of their limitations, Warr and Wall note that:

> We are still left with the feeling that most reported and correlational studies in this area support the conclusion that jobs which offer variety and require the individual to exercise discretion over his work activities, lead to enhanced well being and mental health. Furthermore, the evidence shows how even mundane, machine paced jobs can be redesigned to include greater variety and responsibility (p. 137).

As far as the relationship between job enrichment and productivity is concerned, Lawler (1969), in reviewing the relationship, reports ten studies where both vertical and horizontal enlargement had taken place. In all the studies there were reports of increases in the quality of work but in only four of these was the output significantly improved. Whilst some of the studies suffer from methodological defects, the consistency of the findings points again in the direction of job enrichment affecting productivity, as well as job satisfaction.

Katzell and Yankelovich (1975) also point out the limitations of almost all of the studies produced to date. They also note that some studies fail to find any improvement in job satisfaction or productivity as a result of job enrichment. Of course, a failure to find improvements in satisfaction in a number of studies does not mean that job enrichment, when properly applied, is ineffective. For example, job enrichment applied in an atmosphere of mistrust does not necessarily have implications for situations in which there is established mutual respect. Again, the way job enrichment programmes are carried out may have major effects on the likely outcome. There may well be a failure to show effects of job enrichment where it is 'imposed' from the top, where supervisors are inadequately trained in their new role, or where inappropriate individuals are chosen for the enriched jobs. This does not mean that it cannot be applied successfully where the ground-work for changes has been laid, and where the appropriate principles of job enrichment have been followed.

Katzell and Yankelovich conclude, on the basis of their review, that despite the limitations of many studies, enriched jobs can be more satisfying and that in about 50 per cent of studies considered, aspects of productivity were improved. They suggest that the difference between those studies finding effects and those not, might be in terms of the extent of changes imposed. As noted previously, they argue for a 'critical mass' approach in which only when a large number of changes are made is there likely to be a significant breakthrough in motivation which will affect both job satisfaction and productivity. Small changes, it is claimed, will not be perceived by workers as improving meaningfulness and challenge.

Katzell and Yankelovich also argue that, in addition to the kind of job changes outlined above, hygiene factors must be put in order. If pay is inadequate, for example, the job design changes are liable to be perceived as management's way of avoiding adequate compensation. Pay, however, is not the only factor which might need to be attended to before job design changes are made. Job design changes are unlikely to be accepted if they threaten the individual's security or social relationships.

It certainly appears that the weight of opinion is that job redesign incorporating the principles of job enrichment is beneficial at both a psychological and a financial level. However, as noted previously, in financial terms, the precise nature of the effect of job redesign depends on more than the fact that productivity has increased. It must be shown that profitability has increased in order to justify the expense of redesigning the job and profitability may or may not be related to increased productivity. For this reason, Herzberg (1968) advises that managers should redesign jobs where the investment in industrial engineering does not make the change too costly, where attitudes are poor, where hygiene factors are becoming costly and where motivation will make a difference to performance. Such advice hardly indicates Herzberg to be someone interested in the welfare of workers at the expense of management.

If job enrichment is of such benefit to organisations, the question arises as to why it is not universally adopted. Sirota and Wolfson (1972a) suggest a number of reasons. For example, it is often difficult for managers to translate into practice the theoretical knowledge gained from training courses. Even those with such skills have difficulty in persuading colleagues that job enrichment is likely to improve rather than retard production. Moreover, many managers see job enrichment as an employee benefit rather than as a means of improving productivity and they have still to be persuaded of its financial value. This last point is important as Sirota and Wolfson note that job enrichment is an investment which involves current costs. Like any other investment, it needs to be justified, but unlike many other investments, it cannot easily be shown to be cost beneficial.

Sirota and Wolfson also point to the managerial resistance to change as a factor operating against the implementation of job enrichment programmes. Managers who behave in terms of previously established methods feel safer when things go wrong, and change also carries the implicit assumption that previous methods were not adequate – a fact which few individuals like to admit.

It is not only the manager who may be resistant to change. Many employees are incapable or unwilling to learn new methods of working. Argyris (1976) argues that because working in an enriched job is something alien to many individuals, it is unrealistic to expect acceptance overnight. It might take years before the individual comes to appreciate the advantages of working in an enriched job. Another reason for resistance to changes is put forward by Mars (1977). He points out that where there are informal means of increasing financial rewards, such as by pilfering and theft, there may be 'inexplicable' resistance to job change.

Sirota and Wolfson are not only critical of management and workers: behavioural scientists are seen as being ineffectual in many cases. Many are seen as rigid in their application of one kind of job enrichment programme when studies have shown that various different kinds of approach all have something to offer. Furthermore, they suggest that job enrichment practitioners often appear to have a Messianic zeal which outstrips the realities and benefits of job enrichment and can lead to considerable disappointment. Sirota and Wolfson argue that there are both theoretical and empirical studies which show that job enrichment is likely to be beneficial and studies which show limitations of job enrichment programmes, so that a balanced approach is called for by behavioural scientists if job enrichment is to be taken seriously by management.

How then does the practitioner take account of the various difficulties in implementing job enrichment programmes? Sirota and Wolfson (1972b), Ford (1969), Katzell and Yankelovich (1975) and Hackman *et al.* (1975), amongst others, suggest various procedures.

Katzell and Yankelovich, for example, suggest that eight questions should initially be considered. These steps might be regarded as part of what Sirota and Wolfson and Hackman *et al.* term initial diagnosis.

Katzell and Yankelovich's questions are:

1 *Does the organisation's performance depend substantially on the efforts of its human resources?*

Katzell and Yankelovich argue that service industries are particularly dependent on worker performance although the observation applies to many manufacturing, sales or financial institutions. Indeed, there can be few organisations where it does not apply.

2 *Is the organisation's background of management–employee relationship such that cooperative ventures will be treated seriously?*

Katzell and Yankelovich argue that success depends on a moderate amount of goodwill, especially as things are always liable to go wrong in times of changes.

3 *Does the organisation have a reasonable standard of hygiene factors?*

As Katzell and Yankelovich point out, change is going to be difficult if job security is threatened. Also poor levels of pay may induce feelings of suspicion concerning management's true aims.

4 *Is the technology such that flexibility and change are possible?*

This is probably the most problematic area for management. It is easy to convince oneself that the technological structure is not amenable to change. This may be truer in high technology industries than in other situations but studies have shown how extensive job changes can be made even with seemingly impossible technology. Where a job is so restricted that no change is possible, Warr and Wall argue that it should be abolished by introducing automation. However, in my view, such an approach is not desirable in human terms. If there is one thing worse than a dull job for lowering self-esteem, it is total unemployment.

5 *Is there a genuine interest at the policy-making level in giving equal emphasis to productivity and job satisfaction improvements?*

Only if management is genuinely committed, it is argued, is there any real possibility of success.

6 *Is there a willingness to share the benefits of job enrichment in a tangible form, for example, by increased pay?*

As the study of Locke *et al.* (1976) suggests, for some individuals at least, a failure to reward increased productivity results in dissatisfaction.

7 *Is there a willingness at policy-making level to let go some power so that more decision-making can be devolved downwards?*

As was noted when discussing the need for increasing responsibility, this requires that some decision-making be handed to the individual undertaking an enriched job. This in turn has its problems, in that it can mean job impoverishment for higher levels.

8 *Is the work-force predominantly young, well-educated and possessing or capable of possessing higher levels of skill?*

Katzell and Yankelovich argue that young individuals are more likely to respond to enriched jobs. However, it seems more reasonable to examine the reality of each situation. In any one geographical area, young or educated people may be alienated from particular job enrichment schemes because of prevailing attitudes to work.

Hackman *et al.* (1975) also advocate a job diagnostic stage before any job enrichment changes are implemented. Their job diagnosis involves three aspects, firstly the level of motivation, satisfaction and work performance of employees, secondly the objective characteristics of the job itself and thirdly, the level of needs of employees:

Current levels of motivation, satisfaction and work performance. Many job enrichment programmes are instigated when there appear to be underlying organisational problems. Hackman *et al.* argue that motivation, satisfaction and work performance must be measured to ensure that problems lie here and not in other aspects of the job such as poor design of production systems, and so on.

The characteristics of the job. Hackman *et al.* base their enrichment programme on the four core job aspects of variety, identity, autonomy and feedback, previously investigated by Hackman and Lawler (1971). To this, Hackman *et al.* add a fifth core aspect – job significance. Hackman *et al.* see job variety, significance and identity as contributing to the meaningfulness of the job and task autonomy as contributing to feelings of responsibility. Feeling that the job is high in meaningfulness and responsibility as well as giving feedback on performance results, according to Hackman *et al.*, in high motivation, satisfaction and productivity. Initial job diagnosis, therefore, involves assessing the extent to which particular jobs are high or low on these various core dimensions. By obtaining job profiles along these dimensions, it is possible to see where improvements need to be made.

Level of employee needs. As was noted earlier, not all employees want a job high in the core dimensions. It is necessary, therefore, to assess exactly what needs individuals wish to be satisfied on their jobs. Clearly, only if a significant number of employees wish for job changes allowing for growth, would it be sensible to consider job enrichment changes.

Assuming that the diagnosis indicates that job enrichment is desirable, Hackman *et al.* go on to consider various ways in which the core dimensions of the job can be enriched. These are (1) forming natural work units, (2) combining tasks, (3) establishing client relationships, (4) vertical loading and (5) opening feedback channels.

1 *Forming natural work units.* This consists of two steps, firstly, identifying the basic work units such as 'pages to be typed' for typists in a typing pool, and secondly, grouping items into natural units. For example, in a typing pool, all the pages for a particular member of staff could be typed by one individual instead of assigned at random in the typing pool according to work load. Grouping enables the job to have some identity and significance for the employee, and hence, more meaningfulness.

2 *Combining tasks.* One of the major problems of jobs is that they become so fractionalised and deskilled that little skill is required in the successful completion of the task. By combining tasks so that individuals have a larger cycle from beginning to end, greater job variety is introduced and consequently a greater degree of challenge and skill is required.

3 *Establishing client relationships.* Hackman *et al.* argue that one consequence of fractionalising jobs is that the employee loses contact with the client and hence is less likely to see the significance of what he is doing. By establishing a direct link with clients, employees also receive direct feedback on their perform-

ance. A third core dimension which is improved by direct client relationships is that of job variety. This is likely to increase as the employee has to deal with idiosyncratic client problems which may arise.

4 *Vertical loading.* One way of deskilling a job is to divide the planning, controlling and executing function. The point of vertical loading is seen by Hackman *et al.* as that of partially closing the gap between these functions. Vertical loading might be regarded as the single most important job change as the effect of vertical loading is to increase responsibility (autonomy) and indeed job variety and significance.

Vertical loading involves giving the job-holder greater discretion in setting schedules and work method and checking on quality and training of new employees. It also involves giving additional authority over crisis decisions and assigning priorities.

5 *Opening feedback channels.* As has been noted previously, feedback is necessary if the employee is going to modify and improve his performance. It is also necessary if individuals who are doing well are to be rewarded for good performance (recognition). Hackman *et al.* suggest that frequent feedback is necessary and that job-provided feedback is preferable to only occasional feedback from management. They suggest that steps such as establishing direct client contact often removes feedback blocks. In addition, quality control carried out by those involved in production gives varied and more direct feedback than quality control by remote units. Where possible, of course, supervisors ought to provide information on performance to employees, rather than transmitting such information upwards in secret.

Katzell and Yankelovich consider the question of how job changes such as those recommended by Hackman *et al.* should be introduced. They suggest that it is important to bring employees into future plans from the outset, before any diagnosis, far less change, is introduced. In situations where there is mutual suspicion, it is often useful to employ an external consultant who might well be instrumental in setting up joint management-labour committees to initiate methods of increasing the quality of working life. This can involve presenting joint plans which in turn means devolving influence to lower levels.

Clearly, one early decision which such a joint management–labour committee must make is to institute diagnosis of the kind suggested by Hackman *et al*. One major way of 'cementing' the management–labour committee is to institute investigations and to discuss the findings. Assuming job enrichment is required, various techniques for generating ideas on job change can be utilised. One used by Ford (1969) is brainstorming, which aims at increasing the number of ideas put forward. This technique involves 'greenlighting' where all ideas, however stupid, are listed, and 'redlighting' where such ideas are accepted or rejected in terms of their rationality.

Once the job enrichment changes are decided, great care must be taken in their implementation. Care must be first taken to select the right individuals for the right jobs in terms of their higher order needs and to involve supervisors in job changes. As job enrichment involves major changes in supervisory roles, Murrell (1976) points out that considerable efforts need to be made to educate supervisors in participatory techniques of supervision and to delineate clearly the roles which each individual is expected to perform. It is also necessary to outline clearly the relationship between performance and reward. Furthermore, it is essential to take steps at the outset to ensure that enrichment programmes are evaluated in terms of their success in increasing profitability and the quality of working life, and measures should therefore include quantity and quality of production, absence and turnover as well as job satisfaction, and job involvement. Account must also be taken of the cost of implementing job redesign programmes including the cost of new machinery and the extra management time involved.

SUMMARY

A large number of studies have examined the effects of various means of redesigning jobs. These include job rotation, horizontal job enlargement and job enrichment. Both job rotation and horizontal job enlargement have been criticised as adding little to the challenge of the job and the development and growth of the individual. Furthermore, they are sometimes resented because they disrupt the social rewards of the job.

✳︎Job enrichment aims at more than improving the job satisfaction of the individual which could involve little more than increasing his lower order needs satisfaction. In addition, therefore, the aim is to increase the involvement of the individual in his job by providing him with the potential for psychological growth through the development and application of responsibility and skill. This involves changing the relationship between subordinate and supervisor as well as the structure of the actual job.

A large number of studies have been conducted on the effects of job enrichment. For a variety of reasons they are often extremely difficult to evaluate although many report increased productivity and job satisfaction. There are, however, a number of important limitations. Firstly, not all individuals wish to have an enriched job. Some prefer to have rewards from such factors as social relationships which may be disturbed by reorganisation. Others just do not want to have a challenging job. Secondly, job enrichment threatens the relationship between supervisors and workers because increased responsibility for workers often involves decreased responsibility for supervisors. Thirdly, changes, even when successful in one part of the organisation, may cause disruption in other parts not amenable to job restructuring. Fourthly, jobs differ in the extent to which they are amenable to changes, some kinds of job being more flexible than others. Fifthly, even where job redesign is possible, it may be prohibitively expensive in terms of equipment redesign and actual productivity. Job redesign cannot be considered in isolation from economic constraints. It is worth stressing again, however, that economic consequences involve more than increases in the amount produced. Quality of production, absence and turnover are all reported as being affected by job redesign.

Bearing in mind the many limitations, the evidence on the

beneficial effects of job enrichment is certainly suggestive enough to warrant its serious consideration by managers in most organisations. *possible conclusion.*

8 Concluding Remarks

In the introductory chapter it was pointed out that some investigators of organisational behaviour have doubted the value of the concept of job satisfaction. For example, Davis and Cherns (1975) consider that the current emphasis on job satisfaction is leading to confusion, whilst writers such as Argyris (1976) see the concept as limited in usefulness because so many different factors can be responsible for job satisfaction. Given the many contradictory findings in the field, and the lack of a generally accepted theory of job satisfaction, the reader can be forgiven for agreeing with critics that the field of job satisfaction is vague, contradictory and perhaps, for the most part, common sense.

Such a pessimistic view, however, is not fully justified. Take, for example, the argument that findings on job satisfaction are no more than 'common sense'. One must distinguish between a common sense explanation and a reasonable explanation. Explanations given after the event are invariably seen as reasonable. It is reasonable to account for the fact that there is no relationship between job satisfaction and productivity, for example, by pointing out that people often derive satisfaction in work from aspects of the job that have little to do with productivity, such as from social interactions. Nevertheless, if people are asked what they think is the likely relationship between satisfaction and productivity, before they examine the actual relationship, the great majority will hypothesise that the greater the satisfaction the greater is the productivity. The 'common sense' approach is clearly at variance with what actually happens.

The argument that job satisfaction studies are often contradictory and unhelpful in resolving issues is also an unreasonable argument. Of course it is true that a number of studies in the field of job satisfaction are unsatisfactory in design and interpretation. This is true of most areas of psychology, however, and is not a charge which can be levelled specifically at research into job satisfaction. It is also true that many studies produce contradictory findings. It must be remembered, however, that one is dealing with complex human behaviour in social, organisational and technological situations which vary subtly from study to study. No one study is likely to be an answer to any particular problem. Where contradictory results do emerge, such as in the field of sex differences, then further research has often thrown light on why such inconsistencies are occurring.

As to the charge that job satisfaction studies often produce only vague conclusions, this too is understandable if one considers the complexity of the phenomenon under investigation and the practical difficulties involved in undertaking research. Take the area of job enrichment, for example. Ideally the psychologist might like to set up an experiment in which one group receives an enriched job, another, identical group, an unenriched job and where all other variables such as pay and supervision are controlled. In the real world, however, as in Alderfer's study (1969), management quite naturally wished to employ the 'best' people for new, expensive machinery and felt bound to pay the enriched group more for increased responsibility. Of course, conclusions based on such studies are likely to be vague, but from a practical point of view it is not necessarily of critical importance as long as the combined effect of job changes is to increase productivity and satisfaction.

Rather than demanding the precision of the natural sciences, it seems more reasonable to ask of job satisfaction research whether it has advanced our understanding of the area to any significant extent. My answer would be that it has, and indeed, this advance has sometimes led to discontent with the concept. For example, many studies have shown that there is no direct and simple relationship between job satisfaction and productivity or indeed, between job satisfaction and absence behaviour. Such advances in our knowledge have led writers such as Argyris (1976) to question how useful the concept of job satisfaction is, and has led to a far greater concentration on examining the relationship between different facets of job satisfaction and variables such as productivity and absence. When this kind of approach is used, then different facets of job satisfaction do relate significantly to job aspects such as productivity. Examination of facets of job satisfaction have led to theories of job enrichment, such as those of Hackman *et al.* (1975) discussed in Chapter 7, with a substantial number of studies seeming to support the view that job design changes can lead to improved satisfaction and productivity. Whilst the concept of overall job satisfaction, therefore, might be limited in usefulness in terms of any major relationships with factors of economic importance, this very fact has led to a much more sophisticated approach to understanding the topic. Again, just because overall job satisfaction does not relate well to factors of economic importance, this does not of itself mean that it is of limited usefulness in understanding an individual's reaction to his job. For the individual, how he feels about his job overall is likely to be of critical importance to his wellbeing. How factors such as pay, security and so on relate to this feeling of wellbeing cannot, therefore, fail to be of importance to the study of job satisfaction.

Another justification of studying job satisfaction of course is that it has given rise to numerous findings of practical significance. For example, the study of context factors suggests that employers who wish to avoid problems in this area must pay what is seen as an equitable amount in relation to other individuals with whom the employee compares himself. Research also points to a possible conflict between satisfaction and productivity in that piece-rate schemes are sometimes regarded as less satisfying but nevertheless lead to greater productivity. Researchers such as Warr and Wall (1975) suggest that in order to deal with problems of pay satisfaction a three-tier system be implemented in which pay contains a fixed element, an individual or group incentive element and a company bonus element.

Whilst context factors are undoubtedly of considerable practical significance in relation to job satisfaction, the work on the nature of the job itself has possibly more practical implications.

The findings on job redesign discussed in Chapter 7 show how changes in the nature of the job itself probably affect job satisfaction and productivity. In particular, changes in what Hackman and Lawler (1971) label the four core effects of task variety, autonomy, significance and feedback, when they are improved, appear to lead to improvements in both satisfaction and productivity.

There are, of course, numerous other examples of how the study of job satisfaction has practical applications and many of these have been pointed out in the course of the book. The extensive application of job satisfaction studies to real life problems, together with the light job satisfaction studies have thrown on an understanding of the individual's wellbeing at work, surely justifies continued rigorous study, despite the problems pointed out by critics.

Bibliography

Adams, P. G. and Slocum, J. W. (1971), 'Work group and employee satisfaction', *Pers. Admin.*, 34, 37–43.

Alderfer, C. P. (1969), 'Job enlargement and the organisational context', *Pers. Psychol.*, 22, 418–26.

Alderfer, C. P. (1976), 'Change processes in organisations', in Dunnette, M. D. (ed), *Handbook of industrial and organizational psychology* (Chicago: Rand McNally), pp. 1591–638.

Amaee, S. (1978), 'A social psychological investigation into University students' attitudes to their teachers' function.' Ph.D. Thesis, University College, Swansea.

Amaee, S. and Gruneberg, M. M. (1976), 'Students' knowledge of and attitudes to, the research role of the lecturer', *Research in Education*, 17, 77–82.

Argyle, M., Gardner, G. and Cioffi, I. (1958), 'Supervisory methods related to productivity, absence and labor turnover', *Human Rel.*, 11, 23–40.

Argyris, C. (1964), *Integrating the Individual and the Organisation* (New York: Wiley).

Argyris, C. (1973), 'Personality and organization theory revisited', *Admin. Science Quart.*, 18, 141–67.

Argyris, C. (1976), 'Problems and new directions for industrial psychology' in Dunnette, M. D. (Ed.), *Handbook of Industrial and Organizational Psychology*, (Chicago: Rand McNally), pp. 151–84.

Arvey, R. D., Dewhurst, H. D. and Boling, J. C. (1976), 'Relationship between goal clarity, participation in goal setting, and personality characteristics of job satisfaction in a scientific organisation', *J. Applied Psychol.*, 61, 103–5.

Barrett, G. V. and Bass, B. M. (1976), 'Cross-cultural issues in industrial and organisational psychology' in Dunnette, M. D. (Ed.), *Handbook of industrial and organisational psychology* (Chicago: Rand McNally). pp. 1639–86.

Bartol, K. (1974), 'Sex differences in job orientation: A re-examination', *Proc. of National Academy of Management*, Seattle.

Behling, O. C. (1964), 'The meaning of dissatisfaction with factory work', *Man. of Personnel Quart.*, 3, 11–16.

Blood, M. R. and Hulin, C. L. (1967), 'Alienation, environmental characteristics and worker responses', *J. Applied Psychol.*, 51, 284–90.

Bockman, V. M. (1971), 'The Herzberg controversy', *Pers. Psychol.*, 24, 155–89.

Brayfield, A. H. and Crockett, W. H. (1955), 'Employee attitudes and employee performance', *Psychol. Bull.*, 52, 396–424.

Brief, A. P. and Oliver, R. L. (1976), 'Male-Female differences in work attitudes among retail sales managers', *J. Applied Psychol.*, 61, 526–8.

Campbell, J. P., Dunnette, M. D., Lawler, E. E. and Weik, K. E. (1970), *Managerial Behaviour, Performance and Effectiveness* (New York: McGraw Hill).

Carpenter, H. H. (1971), 'Formal organisational structural factors and perceived job satisfaction of classroom teachers', *Admin. Science Quart.*, 16, 460–5.

Centers, R. and Bugental, D. E. (1966), 'Intrinsic and extrinsic job motivation among different segments of the working population', *J. Applied Psychol.*, 50, 193–7.

Coch, L. and French, J. R. P. (1949), 'Overcoming resistance to change', *Human Rel.*, 1, 512–32.

Cooper, C. L. and Marshall, J. (1976), 'Occupational sources of stress: a review of the literature relating to coronary heart disease and mental ill health', *Brit. J. Occup. Psychol.*, 49, 11–28.

Cooper, R. and Payne, R. (1967), 'Extraversion and some aspects of work behaviour', *Pers. Psychol.*, 20, 45–57.

Cross, D. and Warr, P. (1971), 'Work-group composition as a factor in productivity', *Industrial Relations J.*, 2, 3–13.

Davis, L. E. (1971), 'Job satisfaction research: the post industrial view', *Industrial Relations*, 10, 176–93.

Davis, L. E. and Cherns, A. B. (eds.) (1975), *The Quality of Working Life*, Vol. I., (New York: Free Press).

Dyer, L. and Theriault, R. (1976), 'The determinants of pay satisfaction', *J. Applied Psychol.*, 61, 596–604.

Faunce, W. A. and Dubin, R. (1975), 'Individual investment in working and living' in Davis, L. E. and Cherns, A. B. (eds.), *The Quality of Working Life*, Vol. I, (New York: Free Press), pp. 299–316.

Ferguson, D. (1973), 'A study of occupational stress', *Ergonomics*, 16, 649–64.

Foa, V. G. (1957), 'Relation of workers' expectations to satisfaction with supervisor', *Pers. Psychol.*, 10, 161–8.

Ford, R. N. (1969), *Motivation Through the Work Itself* (New York: American Management Association).

Friedlander, F. and Margulies, N. (1969), 'Multiple inputs of organizational climate and individual value systems upon job satisfaction', *Pers. Psychol.*, 22, 171–83.

French, J. R. P., Israel, J. and As, D. (1960), 'An experiment in participation in a Norwegian factory', *Human Rel.*, 13, 3–19.

Gardner, G. (1977), 'Is there a valid test of Herzberg's two factor theory?' *Brit. J. Occ. Psychol.*, 50, 197–204.

Gebhard, M. E. (1948), 'The effect of success and failure upon the attractiveness of activities as a function of experience, expectation and need', *J. Expt. Psychol.*, 38, 371–88.

Gibson, J. L. and Klein, S. M. (1970), 'Employee attitudes as a function of age and length of service: A reconceptualization', *Academy of Management J.*, 13, 411–25.

Glenn, W. D., Taylor, P. A. and Weaver, C. N. (1977), 'Age and job satisfaction among males and females: A multivariate, multisurvey study', *J. Applied Psychol.*, 62, 189–93.

Goldthorpe, J., Lockwood, D., Bechofer, F. and Platt, J. (1968), *The Affluent Worker* (Cambridge University Press).

Gordon, L. V. (1970), 'Measurement of bureaucratic orientation', *Pers. Psychol.*, 23, 1–11.

Gruneberg, M. M., Startup, R. and Tapsfield, P. (1974a), 'The effect of geographical factors on the job satisfaction of university teachers', *Voc. Asp. of Education*, 26, 25–9.

Gruneberg, M. M., Startup, R. and Tapsfield, P. (1974b), 'A study of university teachers' satisfaction with promotion procedures', *Voc. Asp. of Education*, 26, 53–7.

Gruneberg, M. M. and Startup, R. (1978), 'The job satisfaction of university teachers', *Voc. Asp. of Education*. In press.

Gyllenhammer, P. G. (1977), 'How Volvo adapts work to people', *Harvard Business Review*, 55, 102–13.

Hackman, J. R. and Lawler, E. E. (1971), 'Employee reactions to job satisfaction characteristics', *J. Applied Psychol.*, 55, 259–86.

Hackman, J. R., Oldham, G., Janson, R. and Purdy, K. (1975), 'A new strategy for job enrichment', *California Management Review*, 27.

Hall, D. T., Schneider, B. and Nygren, H. T. (1970), 'Personal factors in organisation identification', *Admin. Science Quart.*, 15, 176–90.

Herzberg, F. (1966), *Work and the Nature of Man* (Cleveland: World Publishing Co).

Herzberg, F. (1968), 'One more time: How do you motivate employees?' *Harvard Business Review*, 46, 53–62.

Herzberg, F., Mausner, B., Peterson, R. O. and Capwell, D. F. (1957), *Job Attitudes: Review of Research and Opinion* (Pittsburgh: Psychological Services of Pittsburgh).

Herzberg, F., Mausner, B. and Snyderman, B. (1959), *The Motivation to Work* (New York: Wiley).

Hespe. G. and Wall, T. (1976), 'The demand for participation among employees', *Human Rel.*, 29, 411–28.

Hill, J. M. M. and Trist, E. L. (1955), 'Changes in accidents and other absences with length of service', *Human Rel.*, 8, 121–52.

Hoppock, R. (1935), *Job Satisfaction* (New York: Harper).

House, R. J. (1971), 'A path goal theory of leader effectiveness', *Admin. Science Quart.*, 16, 321–38.

House, R. J., Filley, A. C. and Kerr, S. (1971), 'Relation of leader consideration and initiating structure to R and D subordinates' satisfaction', *Admin. Science Quart.*, 16, 19–30.

Hulin, C. L. (1966), 'Job satisfaction and turnover in a female clerical population', *J. Applied Psychol.*, 50, 280–5.

Hulin, C. L. and Blood, M. R. (1968), 'Job enlargement, individual differences, and worker responses', *Psychol. Bull.*, 69, 41–65.

Hulin, C. L. and Smith, P. C. (1964), 'Sex differences in job satisfaction', *J. Applied Psychol.*, 48, 88–92.

Hulin, C. L. and Smith, P. C. (1965), 'A linear model of job satisfaction', *J. Applied Psychol.*, 49, 209–16.

Hunt, J. W. and Saul, P. N. (1975), 'The relationship of age, tenure and job satisfaction in males and females', *Academy of management J.*, 690–702.

Ilgen, D. R. and Hollenbach, J. H. (1977), 'The role of job satisfaction in absence behaviour', *Organizational Behaviour and Human Performance*, 19, 148–61.

Iris, B. and Barrett, G. V. (1972), 'Some relations between job and life satisfaction and job importance', *J. Applied Psychol.*, 56, 301–4.

Ivanecevich, J. M. (1976), 'Effects of goal setting on performance and job satisfaction', *J. Applied Psychol.*, 61, 605–12.

Ivanecevich, J. M. and Donelly, J. H. (1975), 'Relation of organizational structure to job satisfaction, anxiety-stress, and performance', *Admin. Science Quart.*, 20, 272–80.

Jenkins, D. C. (1971), 'Psychologic and social precursors of coronary disease (11)', *New England J. of Medicine*, 284, 307–17.

Johnson, T. W. and Stinson, J. E. (1975), 'Role ambiguity, role conflict and satisfaction: moderating effects of individual differences', *J. Applied Psychol.*, 60, 329–33.

Jones, A. P., James, L. R., Bruni, J. R. and Sells, S. B. (1977),

'Black-White differences in work environment perceptions and job satisfaction and its correlates', *Pers. Psychol.*, 30, 5–16.

Kasl, S. V. (1973), 'Mental health and work environment: An examination of the evidence', *J. of Occupational Medicine*, 15, 509–18.

Katzell, R. A. and Yankelovich, D. (1975), *Work, Productivity and Job Satisfaction*, (New York: The Psychological Corporation).

Keller, R. T. (1975),'Role conflict and ambiguity: correlates with job satisfaction and values', *Pers. Psychol.*, 28, 57–64.

Kilbridge, M. (1961), 'Turnover, absence, and transfer rates as indicators of employee dissatisfaction with repetitive work', *Industrial and Labour Relations Review*, 15, 21–32.

King, N. (1970), 'Clarification and evaluation of the two-factor theory of job satisfaction', *Psychol. Bull.*, 74, 18–31.

Klein, S. M. and Maher, J. R. (1966), 'Educational level and satisfaction with pay', *Pers. Psychol.*, 19, 195–208.

Korman, A. K. (1977), *Organisational Behaviour* (Englewood Cliffs: Prentice Hall).

Kornhauser, A. W. (1965), *Mental Health of the Industrial Worker: A Detroit Study* (New York: Wiley).

Kuhlin, R. G. (1963), 'Needs, perceived needs satisfaction and satisfaction with occupation', *J. Applied Psychol.*, 47, 56–64.

Lawler, E. E. (1969), 'Job design and employee motivation', *Pers. Psych.*, 22, 426–35.

Lawler, E. E. (1971), *Pay and Organisational Effectiveness* (New York: McGraw Hill).

Lawler, E. E. (1975), 'Measuring the psychological quality of working life: The why and the how of it', in Davis, L. E. and Clerns, A. B. (eds.), *The Quality of Working Life*, Vol. 1, (New York: Free Press), pp. 123–33.

Lawler, E. E., Hackman, J. R. and Kaufmann S. (1973), 'Effects of job redesign: A field experiment', *J. of Applied Social Psych.*, 3, 49–62.

Lawler, E. E. and O'Gara, P. W. (1967), 'Effects of inequity produced by underpayment on work output, work quality and attitudes towards work', *J. Applied Psych.*, 51, 403–10.

Lawler, E. E. and Porter, L. W. (1969), 'The effect of performance on job satisfaction', *Industrial Relations*, 8, 20–8.

Lewin, K., Lippett, R. and White, R. K. (1939), 'Patterns of aggressive behavior in experimentally created social climates', *J. Social Psych.*, 10, 271–99.

Lischeron, J. A. and Wall, T. D. (1975a), 'Attitudes towards participation among local authority employees', *Human Rel.*, 28, 499–517.

Lischeron, J. A. and Wall, T. D. (1975b), 'Employee participation: An experimental field study', *Human Rel.*, 28, 863–84.

Locke, E. A. (1965), 'The relationship of task success to task liking and satisfaction', *J. Applied Psych.*, 49, 379–85.

Locke, E. A. (1976), 'The nature and causes of job satisfaction' in Dunnette, M. D. (ed.), *Handbook of Industrial and Organisational Psychology* (Chicago: Rand McNally), pp. 1297–1349.

Locke, E. A., Sirota, D. and Wolfson, A. D. (1976), 'An experimental case study of the successes and failures of job enrichment in a government agency', *J. Applied Psych.*, 61, 701–11.

Lodahl, T. M. (1964), 'Patterns of job attitudes in two assembly technologies', *Admin. Science Quart.*, 8, 482–519.

Lodahl, T. M. and Kejner, M. (1965), 'The definition and measurement of job involvement', *J. Applied Psych.*, 49, 24–33.

Lott, A. J. and Lott, B. E. (1965), 'Group cohesiveness as interpersonal attraction', *Psychol. Bull.*, 64, 259–309.

Lyons, T. F. (1972), 'Turnover and absenteeism: A review of relationship and shared correlates', *Pers. Psych.*, 25, 271–81.

McClelland, D. C. (1961), *The Achieving Society* (Princeton, New Jersey: Van Nostrand).

Mangoine, T. W. and Quinn, R. P. (1975), 'Job satisfaction, counter productive behaviour, and drug use at work', *J. Applied Psych.*, 60, 114–16.

Manhardt, P. J. (1972), 'Job orientation of male and female college graduates in business', *Pers. Psych.*, 25, 361–8.

Mann, F. C. and Hoffman, L. R. (1960), *Automation and the Worker* (New York: Holt).

Mann, F. C. and Williams, L. K. (1962), 'Some effects of the changing work environment in the office', *J. of Social Issues*, 18, 92–101.

Mars, G. (1977), 'Some implications of "fiddling" at work'. Paper presented to British Psychological Society Conference, Loughborough.

Maslow, A. H. (1943), 'A theory of human motivation', *Psychological Review*, 50, 370–96.

Metzner, H. and Mann, F. (1953), 'Employee attitudes and absences', *Pers. Psych.*, 6, 467–85.

Mirvis, P. H. and Lawler, E. E. III (1977), 'Measuring the financial impact of employee attitudes', *J. Applied Psych.*, 67, 1–8.

Misshawk, M. J. (1971), 'Supervisory skills and employee satisfaction', *Personnel Administration*, 34, 29–33.

Morse, N. C. and Reimer, E. (1956), 'The experimental change of a major organizational variable', *J. Abnormal and Social Psych.*, 52, 120–9.

Murrell, H. (1976), *Motivation at Work* (London: Methuen).

Newcomb, T. M. (1958), 'Attitude development as a function of reference groups: The Bennington study' in Eleanor E. Maccoby, T. M. Newcomb and E. L. Hartley (eds), *Readings in Social Psychology* (3rd edn), (New York: Holt, Rinehart & Winston), pp. 265–75.

Nicholson, E. A. and Miljus, R. C. (1972), 'Job satisfaction and turnover among liberal arts college professors', *Personnel J.*, 51, 840–5.

Nicholson, N., Brown, C. A. and Chadwick-Jones, J. K. (1976), 'Absence from work and job satisfaction', *J. Applied Psych.*, 61, 728–37.

Nord, W. R. (1977), 'Job satisfaction reconsidered', *American Psychologist*, 32, 1026–35.

Opsahl, R. L. and Dunnette, M. D. (1966), 'The role of financial compensation in industrial motivation', *Psych. Bull.*, 66, 94–118.

Orpen, C. (1974), 'Social desirability as a moderator of the relationship between job satisfaction and personal adjustment', *Pers. Psych.*, 27, 103–8.

Orpen, C. and Ndlovu, J. (1977), 'Participation, individual differences and job satisfaction amongst black and white employees in South Africa', *Int. J. Psych.*, 12, 31–8.

Palmore, E. (1969), 'Predicting longevity: A follow up controlling for age', *The Gerontologist*, 2, 247–50.

Paul, W. J., Robertson, K. B. and Herzberg, F. (1969), 'Job enrichment pays off', *Harvard Business Review*, 47, 61–78.

Payne, R. and Pugh, D. S. (1976), 'Organizational structure and climate', in Dunnette, M. D. (ed), *Handbook of Industrial and Organizational Psychology* (Chicago: Rand McNally), pp. 1125–73.

Porter, L. W. and Lawler, E. E. (1964), 'The effects of "tall" versus "flat" organization structures in managerial job satisfaction', *Pers. Psych.*, 17, 135–48.

Porter, L. W. and Lawler, E. E. (1965), 'Properties of organization structure in relation to job attitudes and behavior', *Psych. Bull.*, 64, 23–51.

Porter, L. W. and Steers, R. M. (1973), 'Organizational, work, and personal factors in employee turnover and absenteeism', *Psych. Bull.*, 80, 151–76.

Pritchard, R. D. (1969), 'Equity theory: A review and critique', *Organisational Behavior and Human Performance*, 4, 176–211.

Pritchard, R. D., Dunnette, M. D. and Jorgenson, D. O. (1972), 'Effects of perceptions of equity and inequity on worker performance and satisfaction', *J. Applied Psychol.*, 56, 75–94.

Pritchard, R. A. and Karasick, B. W. (1973), 'The effects of organizational climate on managerial job performance and job satisfaction', *Organ. Behaviour and Human Performance*, 9, 126–46.

Rabinowitz, S. and Hall, D. T. (1977), 'Organizational research on job involvement', *Psych. Bull.*, 84, 265–88.

Roethlisberger, F. J. and Dickson, W. J. (1939), *Management and the Worker* (Chicago: Harvard University Press).

Ronan, W. A. (1963), 'A factor analysis of eleven job performance measures', *Pers. Psych.*, 16, 255–68.

Sadler, P. J. (1970), 'Leadership style, confidence in management and job satisfaction', *J. Appl. Behav. Science*, 6, 3–19.

Saleh, S. D. and Otis, J. L. (1964), 'Age and level of job satisfaction', *Pers. Psych.*, 17, 425–30.

Schneider, B. and Snyder, R. A. (1975), 'Some relationships between job satisfaction and organisational climate', *J. Applied Psychol.*, 60, 318–28.

Schuler, R. S. (1975), 'Sex, organisation level and outcome importance: Where the differences are', *Pers. Psych.*, 28, 365–75.

Schuler, R. S. (1977), 'Role conflict and ambiguity as a function of the task-structure-technology interaction', *Organ. Behav. and Human Perf.*, 20, 66–74.

Schwab, D. and Cummings, L. L. (1970), 'Theories of performance and satisfaction', *Industrial Relations*, 9, 408–30.

Schwab, D. and Wallace, M. C. (1974), 'Correlates of employee satisfaction with pay', *Industrial Relations*, 13, 78–89.

Scott, R. D. (1972), 'Job expectancy – An important factor in labour turnover', *Pers. J.*, May, 360–3.

Seashore, S. E. (1975), 'Defining and measuring the quality of working life' in Davis, L. E. and Cherns, A. B. (eds.), *The Quality of Working Life*, Vol. I (New York: Free Press) pp. 105–18.

Sexton, W. P. (1968), 'Who calls it psychologically devastating?' *Management of Personnel Quarterly*, 6, 3–8.

Siassi, I., Crocetti, G. and Spiro, H. R. (1975), 'Emotional health, life and job satisfaction in aging workers', *Industrial Gerontology*, 2, 289–96.

Sirota, D. and Wolfson, A. D. (1972a) 'Job enrichment: What are the obstacles?' *Personnel*, 49, 8–17.

Sirota, D. and Wolfson, A. D. (1972b) 'Job enrichment: Surmounting the obstacles', *Personnel*, 49, 4, 8–19.

Slocum, J. W. (1971), 'Motivation in managerial levels: Relationship of need satisfaction to job performance', *J. Applied Psych.*, 55, 312–16.

Slocum, J. W. (1971), 'A comparative study of the satisfaction of American and Mexican operators', *Academy of Management J.*, 14, 89–97.

Smith, P. C. (1955), 'The prediction of individual differences in susceptibility to industrial monotony', *J. Applied Psych.*, 39, 322–9.

Smith, P. C., Kendall, L. M. and Hulin, C. L. (1969), *The Measurement of Satisfaction in Work and Retirement* (Chicago: Rand McNally).

Startup, R. and Gruneberg, M. M. (1973), 'The academic as administrator and policy maker', *Higher Educ. Review*, 6, 45–53.

Steers, R. M. (1975), 'Effect of need for achievement on the job performance – Job attitude relationship', *J. Applied Psych.*, 60, 678–82.

Sussman, G. I. (1973), 'Job enlargement: Effects of culture on worker responses', *Industrial Relations*, 12, 1–15.

Taylor, F. W. (1911), *The Principles of Scientific Management* (New York: Harper).

Trist, E. L. and Bamforth, K. W. (1951), 'Some social and psychological consequences of the Longwall method of coalgetting', *Human Rel.*, 4, 1–38.

Turner, A. N. and Lawrence, P. R. (1965), *Industrial Jobs and the Worker* (Cambridge, Mass.: Harvard University Press).

Van Maanen, J. and Katz, R. (1976), 'Individuals and their careers: Some temporal considerations for work satisfaction', *Pers. Psych.*, 29, 601–16.

Van Zelst, R. H. (1951), 'Worker popularity and job satisfaction', *Pers. Psych.*, 4, 405–12.

Van Zelst, R. H. (1952), 'Validation of a sociometric regrouping procedure', *J. Abnorm. Soc. Psych.*, 47, 299–301.

Vollmer, H. M. and Kinney, J. A. (1955), 'Age, education and job satisfaction', *Personnel*, 32, 38–43.

Vroom, V. H. (1962), 'Ego-involvement, job satisfaction and job performance', *Pers. Psych.*, 15, 159–77.

Vroom, V. H. (1964), *Work and Motivation* (New York: Wiley).

Walker, C. R. and Guest, R. H. (1952), 'The man on the assembly line', *Harvard Business Review*, 30, 71–83.

Wall, T. D. and Stephenson, G. M. (1970), 'Herzberg's two-factory theory of job attitudes: A critical evaluation and some fresh evidence', *Industrial Relations Journal*, 1, 41–65.

Wanous, J. R. (1973), 'Effects of a realistic job preview on job acceptance, job attitudes and job survival', *J. Applied Psych.*, 58, 327–32.

Wanous, J. P. and Lawler, E. E. (1972), 'Measurement and meaning of job satisfaction', *J. Applied Psych.*, 56, 95–105.

Warr, P. and Wall, T. (1975), *Work and Well Being* (Harmondsworth: Penguin).

Weed, S. E., Mitchell, T. R. and Moffitt, W. (1976), 'Leadership style, subordinate personality and task type as predictors of performance and satisfaction with supervision', *J. Applied Psych.*, 61, 58–66.

Weir, M. (ed.) (1976), *Job Satisfaction* (London: Fontana).

Weissenberg, P. and Gruenfeld, L. W. (1968), 'Relationship between job satisfaction and job involvement', *J. Applied Psych.*, 52, 467–73.

Wernimont, P. F. and Fitzpatrick, S. (1972), 'The meaning of money', *J. Applied Psych.*, 56, 218–26.

Wild, R. and Dawson, J. A. (1972), 'The relationship of specific job attitudes with overall job satisfaction and the influence of biographical variables', *J. Management Studies*, 9, 150–7.

Wyatt, S., Langdom, J. N. and Stock, F. G. L. (1937), 'Fatigue and boredom in repetitive work', *Industrial Health Board Report*, 77, Great Britain.

Author Index

Subject Index